HEALTHY PAWS, HAPPY LIFE

A Practical Comprehensive Guide to Dog Health, Nutrition and Wellness

MADDOX MATTHEWS

CONTENTS

INTRODUCTION

There was a chilly autumn morning not so long ago when my old Labrador, Raliegh, seemed to struggle to get up. Concern washed over me as I watched him limp slightly, his usual wagging tail a bit subdued. After a visit to the vet, armed with new knowledge and supplements, we adjusted his diet and exercise routine. Weeks later, watching him run through the park with the joyful abandon of a puppy, I was reminded of the resilience and trust our canine companions place in us and the profound bond we share with them. It was a moment of gratitude and clarity that underscored why I've always felt compelled to give back to him and all the dogs that have been part of our family throughout the years.

Welcome to "Healthy Paws, Happy Life: A Practical Comprehensive Guide to Dog Health, Nutrition and Wellness." This book is not merely a collection of guidelines but a heartfelt compilation drawn from over two decades of firsthand experience treating dogs as cherished family members. My wife and I have navigated the joyful beginnings of puppyhood to the tender challenges of a dog's senior years, always striving to provide our furry companions the best health and happiness.

This book is crafted to be your ultimate guide through the rewarding journey of dog ownership. We cover everything from selecting the perfect companion to understanding the intricacies of canine health, nutrition, and emotional well-being. We delve into the physical and mental aspects of dog care, offering insights into creating a fulfilling environment for your dog at every stage of life.

With over 20 years of experience, my wife and I have explored various facets of canine wellness, from traditional veterinary care to the latest in nutritional science and holistic approaches. This book encapsulates our journey and the lessons learned, providing you with practical advice that combines scientific research with heartfelt experience.

The structure of this book is designed to walk you through every aspect of dog care. It begins with choosing your dog and understanding their health needs, then moves into detailed discussions about nutrition, exercise, and mental health. We've even included a section for you to log and track your dog's health records—a tool we've found indispensable.

Whether you are a first-time dog owner or a seasoned trainer, whether your dog is destined for service, companionship, or family life, there is something here for everyone. We've made sure that the contents of this book cater to the diverse community of dog lovers, ensuring that whether you're caring for a high-energy puppy or a dignified senior, your needs are met.

This guide is built on a foundation of evidence-based information, seasoned with the wisdom that only years of loving and living with dogs can provide. In preparing this book, we've consulted with veterinarians, trainers, and fellow dog owners, ensuring that each page is rich with valuable, actionable information.

As we put together this book, we were guided by extensive research and feedback from dog owners like you. We've tailored this resource to address the real-world questions and concerns that you face, making sure that it's not only informative but also deeply relevant.

In closing, this book is dedicated to all dogs and the people who love them. It's our sincerest wish that the "Healthy Paws, Happy Life: A Practical Comprehensive Guide to Dog Health, Nutrition and Wellness" serves as a trusted companion on your journey, helping your beloved dogs lead the happiest, healthiest lives possible. Here's to many joyful years together with your canine friends.

CHOOSING YOUR CANINE COMPANION

Let me tell you about the day we brought home Sammy, a sprightly Beagle with a penchant for sniffing absolutely everything. Picture us, excited yet clueless about how this little ball of energy would turn our world upside down. Our apartment, perfect for quiet evenings and lazy Sundays, suddenly transformed into Sammy's personal jungle gym. It was then I realized, amid laughter and mild chaos, that understanding our lifestyles and matching them with the right breed was more crucial than we'd ever imagined. This chapter is all about avoiding my mistakes and ensuring you start off on the right paw with your new best friend.

ASSESSING YOUR LIFESTYLE AND CHOOSING THE RIGHT BREED

When diving into the world of dog ownership, it's easy to get swept away by a pair of puppy eyes or a wagging tail. However, the key to a harmonious life with your new furry friend is understanding that each breed comes with its own set of needs and tendencies that may or may not suit your current lifestyle. For instance, consider your typical day-to-day activities and living space before deciding on a breed.

For those of you living in a cozy city apartment, a giant breed like a Great Dane might not be the best choice despite their surprisingly sedate nature. These gentle giants do better in spaces where they can stretch out without knocking over every item in your home. In contrast, smaller breeds like French Bulldogs or Boston Terriers can adapt well to limited living spaces due to their lower exercise requirements. However, it's crucial to consider not just physical space but also the noise factor and your neighbors when your dog decides it's time to sing the songs of their people.

Breed-specific traits also play a massive role in ensuring your home is the right fit for your new companion. High-energy breeds such as Border Collies or Australian Shepherds might find themselves frustrated in an environment where they can't expend their energy positively, leading to destructive behaviors. These breeds thrive in active households where they can participate in agility training and regular hikes or have access to a backyard where they can run to their heart's content.

Moreover, the temperament of a dog is as crucial as their physical needs. Some dogs have a natural affinity for children and make great family pets, while others might prefer a quieter, more predictable environment. For instance, Labrador Retrievers are known for their patient and protective nature towards children, making them an ideal candidate for a bustling family home. In contrast, breeds like the Chow Chow may suit a more adult-only household due to their independent and reserved nature.

Another key aspect for potential and current dog owners to consider is the financial commitment that comes with a pet. This includes not just the initial cost, but also ongoing expenses such as vaccinations, food, and the inevitable unforeseen veterinary bills. A valuable resource we discovered from nearly all consulted sources is the option of pet insurance. Offered by many reputable insurance providers like Nationwide and MetLife, and sometimes available as a benefit through employment, pet insurance can cover a significant portion of costs associated with surgeries, medical procedures, medications, and routine check-ups. The affordability of these plans, typically around $50 per month, complements their value, often paying for themselves annually through reimbursements for medical expenses. In our experience, investing in pet insurance for our dogs has resulted in substantial savings over time.

Lastly, adopting a dog is not just a commitment of space and time but also of heart and resources. Dogs come with a lifelong commitment to their health and happiness. This means considering not only the joys of puppyhood but also the responsibilities that come with caring for a senior dog. Breeds like Golden Retrievers are known to be predisposed to conditions like hip dysplasia, which might entail significant medical care as they age. This long-term perspective ensures you are prepared not just for the fun times but also for the challenges that might arise.

Choosing the right dog breed involves a mix of heart and pragmatism. It requires an honest look at your current lifestyle and an open heart to accommodate your new furry family member's needs. Remember, the goal is to create a loving and sustainable relationship that enriches both your lives for years to come.

THE PROS AND CONS OF PUPPIES VS. ADULT DOGS

When you think about bringing a dog into your home, the image of a playful, stumbling puppy often springs to mind. There's no denying the allure of puppy breath, those mischievous eyes, and the utter joy when they clumsily run towards you. But as adorable as puppies are, they come with a set of needs and challenges that can be as demanding as they are rewarding. Training a puppy is a full-time job that requires a blend of infinite patience, consistent discipline, and a good sense of humor. From housebreaking woes to chewed-up shoes, puppies demand significant time and energy to mold them into well-behaved adult dogs. Socialization is another critical aspect, as those early months are crucial for developing a well-rounded dog that's comfortable with other animals, people, and different environments. The process is akin to laying a foundation for a house; it needs to be done right, but the process can be long and sometimes frustrating, much like waiting for cement to dry while hoping it doesn't rain.

Switching gears, let's consider the often-overlooked option of adopting an adult dog. One of the immediate advantages is bypassing the teething phase and, in many cases, the initial potty training. Many adult dogs in shelters or rescues have lived in homes before, and they often come with a grasp of basic commands and house manners. Their personalities are generally well-formed, so you can get a good read on whether they're a couch potato, a playful adventurer, or a serene companion. This clarity can be incredibly beneficial, allowing you to match your lifestyle and household with the right dog effectively. Moreover, the health history of adult dogs is usually more documented, providing a clearer picture of any existing conditions and what future medical care they might require. This insight can help in budgeting for potential veterinary expenses, which can be less predictable with puppies whose genetic predispositions might not yet be evident.

Emotionally, choosing between a puppy and an adult dog can tug at different heartstrings. Puppies offer the appeal of growing up with you, forming a bond from their formative weeks and integrating deeply into the fabric of your family. There's a certain magic in watching them grow, learning their quirks, and molding their behaviors. On the flip side, adult dogs can form just as profound a bond, often coming from backgrounds that make them immensely appreciative of a second chance at a loving home. They can slot into your life with less fuss and more gratitude, showing affection and loyalty that is just as touching and genuine as that of a puppy.

Both paths have their unique sets of joys and challenges. Whether you find yourself cleaning up a puppy's accidents at dawn or learning the quirks of an older dog, each day brings a mix of trials and triumphs. The decision isn't about which is better universally but which is better for you at this point in your life. Whichever choice you make, the journey with a canine companion is filled with love, learning, and a lot of laughter, ensuring that every effort you put into your furry friend is returned tenfold in unconditional love and companionship.

NAVIGATING THE WORLD OF BREEDERS AND ADOPTION OPTIONS

The decision to welcome a dog into your life is monumental, and how you choose to go about it can shape your experience just as profoundly as the breed you select. If you're considering going through a breeder, it's like looking for a new home— you want the foundation to be solid, ethical, and transparent. A reputable breeder doesn't just love their dogs; they respect the breed and invest heavily in the health and well-being of each pup. They should provide clear documentation of health screenings and be forthcoming about the breeding environment—no dark corners or off-limits areas. These breeders will welcome your questions and should also ask you a fair few, ensuring their puppies are going to a good home. They often remain a resource long after you've brought your puppy home, offering advice and support as your pup grows into adulthood.

Moreover, these breeders partake in health screenings not just as a formality but as a fundamental aspect of their breeding practice. They should be able to provide you with health clearances and test results for genetic conditions known to the breed, ensuring that the likelihood of your puppy inheriting certain diseases is minimized. This kind of transparency isn't just comforting; it's a pillar of responsible breeding that can significantly impact the long-term health of dogs. Additionally, reputable breeders often have a return policy if circumstances change and you can no longer care for the dog. This commitment shows a level of care that goes beyond the transaction—highlighting their dedication to the breed and the individual dogs.

Conversely, adopting from shelters or rescue organizations presents a noble and rewarding path. The benefits of adoption extend beyond the personal joy of saving a life; they ripple out to make a significant impact on the broader issue of animal homelessness. Shelters and rescues are often populated by dogs who have been abandoned or surrendered—not because they're flawed, but because their previous owners couldn't, or wouldn't, provide for them. By choosing adoption, you're not only giving a dog a second chance, but you're also making space for another needy animal to have the same opportunity. Cost-wise, adoption generally involves a lower upfront investment than purchasing from a breeder. The fees you pay are used to support the shelter, helping other animals receive the care they need and deserve.

Breed-specific rescues occupy a unique niche in the adoption landscape. These organizations cater to specific breeds, offering a wealth of specialized knowledge about their care, behavior, and health needs. If you're drawn to a particular breed but want to adopt, these rescues are a goldmine. They provide the expertise of a breeder with the ethos of a rescue, ensuring that the dogs receive the best of both worlds: a breed-savvy approach in a non-commercial setting. These rescues often work with dogs that have been evaluated in foster homes, giving you a clearer picture of how they might fit into your life.

Navigating the legal and ethical landscape of dog ownership is also crucial. Understanding the laws that govern pet ownership in your area, such as licensing requirements, leash laws, and noise ordinances, can prevent legal headaches down the road. Ethically, the choice between a breeder and adoption can weigh heavily. The decision to support responsible breeders contributes to the overall health and vitality of breeds while opting to adopt can address the pressing issues of overpopulation and euthanasia in shelters. Both paths offer the opportunity to make a difference—the right choice depends on a blend of personal compatibility and ethical consideration.

Choosing how and where you get your dog is a deeply personal decision that sets the stage for your future together. Whether through a diligent, loving breeder or an adoption route that saves a life, the commitment remains the same: to provide a loving forever home to a deserving dog. As you navigate these options, consider not only what you can offer to your new companion but also what this choice says about the broader implications of dog ownership. Your decision has the power to echo beyond your individual story, influencing the lives of many dogs and the people who love them.

UNDERSTANDING HEALTH CERTIFICATIONS AND THEIR IMPORTANCE

Imagine you're investing in a car. You wouldn't just look at the shiny exterior and make a decision; you'd probably want to check under the hood, understand the vehicle's history, and ensure it's in top shape. Similarly, when choosing a puppy or a breed, health certifications play a crucial role, much like a vehicle's service records. These certifications are not just pieces of paper; they are reassurances that the breeder has done their due diligence in minimizing the risk of genetic health problems that can affect your dog's life and your heart.

Health certifications are vital indicators of a dog's genetic health. They involve various tests conducted by qualified veterinarians to check for specific genetic disorders that are prevalent in certain breeds. For instance, hip dysplasia, a common skeletal condition often found in larger breeds like German Shepherds and Labradors, can be screened through certifications like those from the Orthopedic Foundation for Animals (OFA). Similarly, progressive retinal atrophy, which can lead to blindness, is another condition that breeders test for in breeds like Cocker Spaniels and Labrador Retrievers. By ensuring these certifications are in place, breeders can not only breed out these conditions over generations but also provide potential owners with transparency and peace of mind regarding the puppy's health.

The importance of breeder transparency cannot be overstated. A responsible breeder will be proud to show you the health certifications of the puppy's parents and explain what those certifications mean. They ensure that each breeding decision is made with the health and well-being of the puppies in mind. However, red flags should go up if a breeder hesitates to show health documentation or seems evasive about their breeding practices. Such signs can indicate that the breeder may not have conducted the necessary health tests, potentially leading to a higher risk of health issues in their puppies. Always remember, a trustworthy breeder's openness is as crucial as the health tests themselves.

Connecting these dots, the impact of health certifications on a dog's long-term health is significant. Investing in a puppy with a clear health certification might cost more upfront, but it's akin to choosing a path with fewer obstacles. These early investments in health checks can prevent numerous issues that might require expensive treatments later on. For example, the cost of surgery for hip dysplasia can run into thousands of dollars, not to mention the potential pain and decreased quality of life for your dog. On the other hand, a puppy cleared for genetic hip issues through OFA certification significantly reduces such risks, ensuring a healthier, happier life alongside fewer vet visits.

Furthermore, the cost implications of opting for health-certified dogs are like choosing a well-maintained car over one that might save you money initially but could break down any minute, costing more in long-term repairs. A non-certified dog might have a lower purchase price, but the gamble on potential genetic health problems can lead to high medical bills and heartache. It's an investment in peace of mind, knowing that you've done everything possible to ensure your furry companion lives a long, healthy life free from preventable genetic ailments.

When you stand in a breeder's home, surrounded by the joyful chaos of wagging tails and puppy kisses, remember that the joy of choosing a new companion comes with responsibilities. Ensuring that health certifications are in order, understanding their implications, and recognizing the signs of a transparent, responsible breeder are all steps on the path to welcoming a healthy, happy dog into your life.

PREPARING YOUR HOME FOR A NEW DOG

Bringing a new dog into your home is like setting the stage for a great play; everything needs to be in place before the curtain rises. Think of your home as a theater where your new dog will play out their days in comfort and safety. The first step is creating a space that's both welcoming and secure. Start by dog-proofing your home, much like you'd baby-proof it for a toddler. Secure electrical cords out of reach, ensure that small objects that could be swallowed are off the floor, and put away any toxic plants or chemicals. Consider a dedicated space for your new arrival; somewhere they can retreat to when the world feels a bit too much. This could be a cozy corner with a crate, open and inviting, lined with a soft bed and some toys. It's their sanctuary, a place where they can observe and settle in at their own pace.

Now, let's talk essentials. Before your dog sets a paw inside their new home, you'll want to have a few key supplies on hand. First up, food and water dishes. Stainless steel or ceramic are good choices as they're easy to clean and hard to tip over. Next, bedding. Invest in a good-quality bed that matches your dog's size; this will be their snooze zone, a place they can curl up and dream of chasing squirrels. Toys are a must-have, not just for fun but for mental and physical stimulation. Include a mix of chew toys, balls, and interactive toys to keep them engaged when you're not around. Don't forget grooming supplies. Even if your dog is a short-haired breed, a basic grooming kit that includes a brush, nail clippers, and dog shampoo is essential for their well-being.

Establishing a routine is crucial from day one. Dogs, much like humans, find comfort in predictability. Feeding at regular times, scheduled walks, and structured playtime can significantly ease your dog's transition into their new environment. This routine doesn't just help with house training but also sets the tone for your dog's behavior. Consistent feeding times regulate their digestion and help manage their energy levels, while regular walks and playtime provide the exercise and mental stimulation they need to stay healthy and happy. Remember, a tired dog is a good dog. Regular exercise helps to burn off excess energy that might otherwise be channeled into less desirable behaviors like chewing or excessive barking.

Integrating your new dog into a household with existing pets or family members is somewhat like choreographing a dance. Everyone has to move in sync, and timing is everything. If you have other pets, introductions should be done gradually and on neutral territory if possible. Start with short, controlled meetings that allow the animals to sniff and explore each other without the pressure of immediate cohabitation. Use positive reinforcement to reward calm, non-aggressive behavior. For introductions to human family members, especially children, it's crucial to teach gentle handling and respect for the dog's space. Young children should be supervised to ensure they don't inadvertently hurt the dog and prevent it from becoming too overwhelmed. Remember, every interaction your dog has in these early days should be positive and reassuring, reinforcing their sense of security and helping them understand that they are in a safe, loving environment.

As you set up your home, gather the essential items, and establish routines, keep in mind that patience and consistency are your best tools. Every dog settles in at their own pace and needs time to adjust to their new surroundings and family. Some might feel at home within a few days, while others might take weeks to really start showing their true personality. Give them the space and support they need to feel secure, and before you know it, they'll be ruling the roost, and you'll wonder how you ever lived without them.

NUTRITION FOR EVERY LIFE STAGE

Picture this: your lively puppy, with boundless energy, suddenly morphs into a dignified senior dog, preferring leisurely strolls to frantic frolics. Just as their activity levels change, so too do their dietary needs. Navigating these shifts can feel a bit like trying to solve a puzzle with pieces that keep changing shapes. But fear not! Understanding the nutritional journey from puppyhood to their golden years is less about finding perfect solutions and more about making adaptable, informed choices that support your dog's health at every stage.

NUTRITIONAL NEEDS FROM PUPPIES TO SENIORS

Understanding Life Stage Requirements

From the moment a puppy tumbles into your life, nutrition plays a pivotal role in their growth and development. These little bundles of joy require a diet rich in proteins and fats to support their rapid growth and high energy levels. Imagine these nutrients as the building blocks and fuel needed to construct their tiny bodies into healthy adult dogs. However, as your dog ages, their metabolic rate slows down, mirroring their more sedentary lifestyle. This shift means that the rich diet that once fueled endless games of fetch might now lead to unwanted weight gain. Thus, transitioning to an adult-specific formula that maintains muscle mass while preventing obesity is crucial.

When your dog enters their senior years, their diet may need another adjustment. Older dogs often face challenges such as decreased kidney efficiency and joint issues. This is where the magic of diet adaptation comes into play. For instance, incorporating foods high in omega fatty acids can support joint health, reduce inflammation, and ease pain. Additionally, reducing calorie intake can help manage their weight, which is particularly important as their ability to exercise diminishes. It's like tweaking the ingredients of a well-loved recipe to better suit the changing taste preferences of an aging family member—done out of love and a deep understanding of their needs.

Protein and Fat Ratios

Let's dive a bit deeper into the world of proteins and fats. For your energetic puppy, these nutrients are akin to a fuel mix that powers a high-performance engine—essential for their growth spurts and energy bursts. High-quality proteins help build strong muscles, while fats provide a concentrated source of energy that keeps them playful and engaged. However, as your dog ages, their nutritional "engine" prefers a different mix, one that maintains their health without overtaxing their system. This means slightly reducing the fat content to prevent weight gain and adjusting protein levels to maintain, but not overly increase, muscle mass. It's a bit like changing the gears on a bike; you need to find the right gear that matches the terrain—too high, and pedaling becomes a chore; too low, and you may not move as efficiently as you need.

Special Nutritional Considerations for Age

As your dog transitions through life's stages, special dietary considerations become the linchpins in managing their health. For instance, senior dogs might benefit from diets that support renal health, especially if they show signs of kidney stress. This could involve lower protein diets that are easier on their kidneys, paired with increased hydration to help flush toxins. Additionally, enhancing their diet with antioxidants such as vitamins E and C can combat age-related oxidative stress, keeping their cells healthier for longer. It's akin to tuning up an old, beloved car—while it might not race like it used to, with the right care, it can still offer a smooth, enjoyable ride.

Frequency and Portion Size Adjustments

Managing how much and how often your dog eats is crucial throughout their life. Puppies often require several small meals a day to manage their incredible energy needs without overloading their tiny stomachs. It's like fueling up a race car; frequent pit stops are necessary to finish the race. As your dog matures, the number of meals can decrease, but the precision in portion size becomes paramount to avoid overfeeding. Senior dogs, with their reduced energy expenditure, benefit from smaller, nutrient-dense meals that cater to their slower lifestyle. Adjusting meal sizes and frequencies is not just about keeping them physically healthy but also about enhancing their overall quality of life, ensuring every meal is a step towards longevity.

Navigating your dog's dietary needs through different life stages doesn't have to be a daunting task. With a clear understanding of their changing requirements and a bit of vigilance, you can ensure that their diet supports a long, happy life. Think of yourself as the expert chef who knows just when to adjust the heat, change the ingredients, or tweak the recipe to make sure the meal is always just right. Whether they're bounding around as puppies or sauntering through their senior years, your knowledge and care can make all the difference in their health and happiness.

READING AND UNDERSTANDING DOG FOOD LABELS

Ever feel like deciphering a dog food label is like trying to understand a foreign language? You're not alone. Let's break down this cryptic code together, starting with the ingredient list. Picture yourself in the grocery aisle, bag of dog food in hand, surrounded by choices claiming to be the best for your beloved pup. The first thing to look at is the order of ingredients—because, just like in your favorite recipes at home, the order matters. Ingredients are listed by weight, which means the first few ingredients make up the bulk of the food. If you see a whole meat (like chicken or beef) at the top, you're off to a good start. However, if there's a "by-product" up there, you might want to think twice.

Now, "by-products" aren't necessarily the villains some make them out to be. They're often parts of the animal that humans prefer not to eat, like organs and bones, which can be nutritious. But quality varies wildly, so they're a bit of a gray area. What you really want to watch out for are vague descriptions like "meat meal" or "animal fat." These terms can come from any number of sources, and not all of them are good. It's like getting a mystery meal at a restaurant; it could be delicious, or it could be a disaster—you just don't know.

Moving on to the nutrients, the big players are proteins, fats, and carbohydrates, along with a supporting cast of vitamins and minerals. High-quality proteins from meat, fish, or eggs should be high on the list because they provide the amino acids that are vital for your dog's health. Fats should come from identifiable sources too, like chicken fat or salmon oil, rather than generic "animal fat." They're important for energy and cell integrity and as carriers for fat-soluble vitamins. Carbohydrates provide energy and come from sources like grains, legumes, and vegetables. While dogs don't technically need carbs, they can be a good source of fiber and other nutrients.

Navigating the maze of health claims on dog food packages can feel like walking through a minefield. Words like "natural," "holistic," and even "organic" have specific legal definitions that might not align with common sense interpretations. For instance, "natural" can still include synthetic vitamins and minerals. When you see these terms, check for certifications that back them up, like the USDA Organic seal or verification from the Association of American Feed Control Officials (AAFCO). These certifications mean that the food meets specific standards and isn't just marketing fluff.

Lastly, let's talk about the different types of dog food—dry, wet, raw, and dehydrated. Each has its pros and cons. Dry food is convenient and helps keep teeth clean, but it often contains more carbohydrates and fewer fresh ingredients. Wet food is excellent for hydration and palatability, which can be perfect for picky eaters, but it can be pricier and less convenient than kibble. Raw diets offer a back-to-nature appeal and can include fresher ingredients but require careful handling to avoid bacterial contamination.

Dehydrated food strikes a balance by offering minimally processed ingredients with the convenience of dry food, though it can also be on the expensive side.

Choosing the right food for your dog is a bit like selecting the right school for a child—it needs to meet their nutritional needs and fit into your lifestyle. By understanding how to read and interpret dog food labels, you can make informed decisions that ensure your pup gets the nutrition they need to thrive. Remember, the best choice is one that combines quality ingredients with balanced nutrition tailored to your dog's age, health, and preferences. So next time you're staring down that dog food aisle, take a deep breath—you've got this.

HOMEMADE MEALS AND RECIPES FOR OPTIMAL HEALTH

Imagine transforming your kitchen into a little chef's corner for your furry friend, where every meal is crafted with love, care, and a dash of fun. The beauty of homemade dog food lies not just in its freshness but in the control it gives you over what goes into your dog's bowl. For dogs with specific dietary needs or health issues, this control is not just beneficial; it's a game-changer. By preparing meals at home, you sidestep the myriad of preservatives found in commercial dog foods. More importantly, you get to handpick ingredients, ensuring each meal is free from fillers and additives that could aggravate certain health conditions. Think of it as tailoring a suit—it needs to fit perfectly to look good and feel comfortable, and with homemade meals, you're ensuring your dog's diet fits their health requirements precisely.

However, diving into homemade dog food requires a balance as delicate as a soufflé—if the nutritional balance is off, the results can be less than desirable. To ensure your dog's diet remains complete and balanced, integrating a variety of proteins, carbohydrates, and fats is crucial. Each meal should be a little symphony of nutrients playing together harmoniously. For instance, a combination of lean meats, healthy fats, and digestible carbohydrates provides the energy and building blocks your dog needs. But it's not just about throwing ingredients together; understanding the nutritional value of each component and how they complement each other is vital.

Now, let's roll up our sleeves and get into some sample recipes. For the young, energetic puppy, a protein-rich meal is vital for growth and development. A simple chicken and rice dish could be the way to go. Start with some diced chicken breast, cook it until it's nicely browned, and then mix it with cooked rice and a medley of vegetables like carrots and peas—softened to be gentle on those tiny teeth. For an adult dog, you might want to mix things up a bit —perhaps a beef and sweet potato feast enriched with flaxseeds for that shiny coat we all love to see. As for the seniors, a turkey and pumpkin purée with a sprinkle of green beans can provide a lower-calorie, high-fiber meal that supports digestion and joint health.

Transitioning your dog to homemade food is much like introducing a new character into a well-loved book series—it needs to be done gradually and thoughtfully. Start by mixing a small amount of the homemade meal with their current dog food, slowly increasing the homemade portion over a week or so. This gradual introduction helps prevent digestive upsets and allows your dog's system to adjust to the new diet. It's like easing into a hot bath; it's all about comfort and taking it one step at a time.

As you embark on this journey of homemade dog nutrition, remember, each meal is an opportunity to enhance your dog's health and deepen the bond you share through the care and thought put into their food. It's not just about feeding them; it's about nurturing them.

THE ROLE OF SUPPLEMENTS IN CANINE NUTRITION

When you think about supplements, you might picture a shelf filled with bottles and jars that promise everything from shinier coats to boundless energy. But just like us, our furry companions sometimes need a little extra nutritional boost to tackle specific health issues or to enhance their overall well-being. It's a bit like tuning a musical instrument—sometimes, you need to adjust a string here and there to hit the perfect note.

Let's consider the scenarios where supplements are not just helpful but necessary. For instance, as dogs age, their joints might get a bit creaky. It's not unlike watching your favorite childhood swing set rust over time; it squeaks a bit more and doesn't move as smoothly. Here, supplements like glucosamine and chondroitin can be a real game changer, acting like a can of oil for that old swing set, helping to lubricate those joints and ease the discomfort. Or perhaps your dog has a dull coat and dry skin, signs that can indicate a deficiency in essential fatty acids. Adding fish oil or flaxseed oil can bring back that glossy shine to their coat, much like using conditioner on dry hair.

Moving on to the selection process, choosing the right supplement is akin to finding the perfect pair of walking shoes; it needs to fit well and be of good quality to do the job right. Start by looking for brands that have a strong reputation for quality and transparency. These brands often invest in clinical research and rigorous testing to back up their health claims. Trustworthy brands will also be clear about the source of their ingredients, ensuring they are ethically sourced and sustainably produced. Ingredients should be as natural as possible, without unnecessary fillers or artificial additives. It's like comparing a homemade meal to fast food; the quality of ingredients matters immensely.

However, while supplements can offer significant benefits, there's a line that can be easily crossed into over-supplementation. It's similar to overwatering a plant; though well-intentioned, too much water can drown the roots and stunt the plant's growth. For dogs, excessive intake of certain vitamins and minerals can lead to conditions like vitamin toxicity or interfere with the absorption of other essential nutrients. For example, too much calcium can lead to bone problems in large-breed puppies, while excessive vitamin A can cause dehydration and joint pain. Always follow the recommended dosages on the label or a dosage advised by your vet. Think of it as a recipe; for the best results, you need to stick to the measurements.

Integrating supplements into your dog's diet should be done with the finesse of blending a smoothie—everything should mix seamlessly. If the supplement comes in a pill form, it can be mixed into their regular meals to mask the taste, especially if your dog is a bit picky. Powders have a similar flexibility and can be sprinkled over their food like a seasoning, adding a nutritional boost without much fuss. Liquid forms of supplements can be mixed into wet food or a small amount of broth, making it an easy addition to their diet. Remember, the key is to integrate these supplements in a way that maintains the meal's palatability and ensures that your dog consumes the full dose, getting all the intended health benefits without any mealtime drama.

By understanding when supplements are necessary, selecting the right products, and integrating them into your dog's diet with care, you can effectively support their health and vitality. Whether it's easing their joint pain, improving their digestive health, or giving their coat a little extra shine, the right supplements can make a significant difference in their quality of life. It's about giving them the best care possible, with every meal and every supplement serving as an expression of your love and commitment to their well-being.

2.5 Managing Diet for Dogs with Allergies and Sensitivities

Imagine your dog as a guest at a dinner party where, unfortunately, some of the dishes cause a bit of a tummy upset. Just like us, our canine friends can have allergies and sensitivities that make certain common ingredients a no-go. Common culprits in the doggy world include beef, dairy, and wheat—foods that are often staples in dog diets but can sometimes lead to itchy skin, digestive woes, and other uncomfortable reactions. Spotting these signs of allergies in your dog can be as straightforward as noticing when they excessively scratch themselves after meals, display gastrointestinal upset regularly, or even suffer from chronic ear infections.

Navigating this can feel a bit like being a detective in a culinary mystery, but with a strategic approach, you can pinpoint the exact cause. This is where an elimination diet comes into play. Think of it as peeling back the layers of your dog's diet until you hit the core. Start by stripping down their meals to basics—usually a protein and carbohydrate that they've never had before, like duck and potatoes. This baseline diet should be maintained for a few weeks, and it's crucial during this period to ensure that your dog doesn't eat anything outside of the designated meal plan—yes, that means those sad puppy eyes will just have to miss out on table scraps and treats for a while. After their symptoms have cleared, you'll begin to reintroduce the old foods one at a time, with a span of a few weeks between each. If symptoms flare up after adding a particular ingredient, you've likely found the culprit.

For those of us who'd rather skip the kitchen experiments, hypoallergic dog food options can be a godsend. These are specially formulated to include hydrolyzed proteins—proteins broken down into small pieces that the immune system doesn't recognize as allergens—or novel proteins that your dog hasn't been exposed to. This switch can often lead to a dramatic improvement in allergy symptoms, making meal times happy times once again.

However, managing a dog's food sensitivities is often a long-term commitment. Regular check-ups with your vet become part of your routine, helping you tweak the diet as needed and ensure your furry friend stays in tip-top shape. It's all about maintaining that perfect balance—keeping them happy and healthy while managing their dietary needs. It's not just about the right now, but ensuring they have a full, vibrant life without the constant discomfort that allergies can bring.

In wrapping up this exploration of canine dietary needs, remember that every dog is as unique as a thumbprint. What works for one might not work for another, even within the same household. Whether you're navigating puppyhood or managing a mature dog's health, staying informed and responsive to their changing dietary needs will help ensure they remain your happy and healthy companion for years to come. As we close this chapter on nutrition, we pave the way to understanding another critical aspect of dog care—training and behavior, ensuring that your journey with your canine companion is as smooth and joyful as possible.

COMPREHENSIVE TRAINING TECHNIQUES

Picture this: It's a sunny Saturday morning, and there you are, in the backyard, armed with a pocketful of treats and a brand new leash, ready to embark on the noble quest of training your vivacious puppy. The scene is set; your pup's tail is wagging like a metronome on overdrive, and you think to yourself, "How hard can it be?" Cut to twenty minutes later, and it's chaos—treats are strewn about, the leash is tangled, and your pup is more interested in chasing butterflies than listening to your commands. It's a comedy of errors, but beneath the surface, it's your first step into the profound, sometimes perplexing world of dog training.

BASIC TRAINING TO MASTERY: LAYING THE FOUNDATION

Essential Commands

Training your dog starts with mastering the basics. These fundamental commands aren't just tricks; they are essential tools that facilitate communication between you and your furry friend, ensuring their safety and your sanity. Let's break down these cornerstone commands:

- **Sit**: This is often the first command taught, and for good reason. It's simple, and it creates a baseline for calm behavior.
- **Stay**: Crucial for safety, 'stay' teaches your dog self-control and patience.
- **Come**: Possibly the most important in terms of safety, 'come' can bring your dog back to you if they head towards danger.
- **Heel**: This keeps your dog walking nicely on a leash without pulling you down the street.
- **Down**: It's a submissive posture that can help mitigate dominant behavior and promote calmness.

Each of these commands serves as a building block for more complex interactions and ensures that your dog can participate fully and safely in a variety of situations.

Techniques for Teaching Commands

Now, teaching these commands effectively often involves a sprinkle of patience, a dash of strategy, and a generous heap of consistency. Positive reinforcement is the chef's kiss in dog training. Here's a step-by-step breakdown to whip up a perfect training session:

1. **Choose the Right Treats**: High-value treats can make the training process smoother. These are treats your dog goes bananas for and are usually reserved for training sessions to maintain their 'special' status.

2. **Keep Sessions Short and Sweet**: Dogs have short attention spans. Training sessions should be short, focused bursts of fun, around 5-10 minutes long.

3. **Be Clear and Consistent**: Use clear, consistent commands. If you use "come" one day and "come here" the next, you might just end up confusing your dog.

4. **Reward Promptly**: Timing is everything. Reward your dog the instant they obey the command. This helps them associate the action with the reward.

Importance of Early Training

Starting training early sets a puppy up for success by instilling good habits from the get-go. Early training not only socializes a puppy to various environments and individuals but also helps prevent the development of undesirable behaviors. Think of it as setting the right tone from the first note in a long symphony—the melody just flows more smoothly.

Setting the Training Environment

Creating the right environment for training is like setting the stage for a great performance. It should be quiet, free from distractions, and safe. A familiar, controlled environment allows your dog to focus on the tasks at hand without the world pulling their attention away. As they become more proficient, they gradually introduce more distractions. This enhances their ability to follow commands in different situations, ensuring that their training holds up whether they're in a calm living room or a bustling park.

Training your dog is more than teaching them how to behave; it's about nurturing a relationship built on mutual respect and understanding. It's about those quiet moments when they nail a command and look at you with eager eyes and a wagging tail as if saying, "What's next?" It's these foundations that pave the way for a harmonious and joyful life together, filled with respect, love, and a deep bond that only grows stronger with each training session.

ADVANCED TRAINING TECHNIQUES FOR MENTAL STIMULATION

Imagine your dog's training routine as a playground where each new trick and command adds a fun, challenging element to the landscape. Once you and your canine companion have mastered the basics, it's time to elevate the game. Advanced commands and tricks do more than just impress your friends; they keep your dog's mind sharp and their body agile. Think of it as adding a few brain-teasers to keep the workout interesting for both of you.

Starting with something like 'roll over' can be a delightful party trick but also a great way to enhance your dog's physical flexibility and obedience. To teach this, start by asking your dog to lie down. Hold a treat by their nose and slowly move it towards their shoulder, encouraging them to roll over to follow it. Praise them enthusiastically when they complete the roll and offer the treat. This trick, while simple, encourages your dog to follow complex commands and trust your guidance through unfamiliar movements.

Fetch, beyond its fun facade, is excellent for teaching impulse control and retrieval skills. It starts with training your dog to understand what it means to 'take it' and 'drop it,' which are commands that lay the groundwork for controlled retrieve. These commands ensure that your dog knows how to pick up items gently without damaging them and to release them on command, which can be particularly useful in everyday situations, like when they grab something they shouldn't have.

For those with a more adventurous spirit, agility training can be particularly stimulating. Setting up an agility course in your backyard or joining a local club can offer your dog a fantastic array of physical challenges. Weaving through poles, jumping over hurdles, and navigating through tunnels doesn't just tire them out physically but also provides a mental workout as they learn to follow complex commands quickly and accurately. Agility training strengthens your communication with your dog, as each obstacle requires guidance to be completed correctly.

The beauty of these advanced training techniques lies in their dual benefit: they keep your dog engaged and help deepen the bond between you. Each new trick learned and every obstacle overcome adds layers of trust and understanding, reinforcing your role as a guide and their confidence in following your lead.

Using Puzzle Toys and Games

Now, let's talk about those rainy days when an outdoor adventure isn't on the cards. This is where puzzle toys and games come into play, turning a potentially boring day into a stimulating experience for your dog. Interactive toys, such as puzzle feeders, treat-dispensing games, and hide-and-seek toys, are fantastic for mental stimulation. They challenge your dog to solve problems, which can help improve their cognitive abilities and keep them mentally sharp.

Imagine a toy that requires your dog to move a series of sliders to find a hidden treat. Each slider might represent a small puzzle piece, and the treat is the reward for solving the puzzle. These toys mimic the challenges dogs might face in the wild, like foraging for food, which can be incredibly satisfying and mentally enriching for them. The act of solving the puzzle for a reward also mimics the training environment, where they learn through positive reinforcement, making these toys an extension of their training sessions.

Integrating these toys into your dog's daily routine can help prevent boredom and the behaviors that come with it, such as excessive chewing or barking. They keep your dog's brain engaged, turning potentially destructive energy into a positive outlet. Plus, setting up these games for your dog can be a fun way to observe their problem-solving approach, giving you insights into their personality and preferences.

Incorporating Training into Daily Activities

Training doesn't have to be a session that starts and stops with a command. It can seamlessly weave into the fabric of your daily life, turning routine activities into opportunities for reinforcement and learning. For instance, asking your dog to sit before meals reinforces patience and impulse control daily. During walks, random sit-stay commands can improve their obedience and focus amid distractions. Even a game of fetch can be turned into a training session, reinforcing commands like 'come,' 'drop it,' or 'stay' in a fun and dynamic setting.

This approach ensures that training is not seen as a task but as a part of life, keeping your dog consistently engaged. It also helps reinforce behaviors until they become second nature, reducing the need for formal sessions over time. By integrating training into daily activities, you ensure your dog's skills remain sharp, and their behavior remains consistent, no matter the setting.

Benefits of Continuous Learning

Continual learning is as beneficial for dogs as it is for humans. It keeps their minds active and their skills sharp, but more importantly, it significantly enhances the bond between you. Each training session is an opportunity to understand each other better, building a deeper level of mutual trust and communication.

The benefits extend beyond the immediate joys of a well-trained dog. Mentally stimulated dogs are generally happier and healthier. They are less likely to develop behavioral issues and can adapt more easily to new situations and commands. Moreover, the mental engagement provided by continuous learning can contribute to better mental health, keeping age-related cognitive decline at bay.

By committing to continuous learning and advanced training, you're not just training a dog; you're raising a companion who is well-adjusted, confident, and deeply bonded to you. This ongoing commitment to their development is a testament to the depth of your relationship, ensuring that you both continue to grow and learn together in a dynamic, mutually rewarding way.

ADDRESSING COMMON BEHAVIORAL ISSUES

Imagine you're enjoying a peaceful evening at home, perhaps curled up with a good book or catching up on your favorite series, when suddenly, your serene bubble is burst by the sound of incessant barking. Or maybe you've come home to find your new shoes transformed into a chewed mess. These scenarios are not just disruptions to your calm environment; they're signs that your furry companion is trying to tell you something. Understanding and addressing common behavioral issues in dogs is much like decoding a message without a cipher—it requires patience, keen observation, and a bit of know-how.

Identifying Behavioral Problems

Barking, chewing, and aggression are among the most prevalent behavioral issues in dogs, and each behavior has its roots in various causes. Excessive barking, for instance, can stem from anxiety, excitement, attention-seeking, or even as a response to environmental triggers like loud noises or unfamiliar people. Similarly, destructive chewing often points to anxiety, boredom, or the lack of appropriate chew toys. Aggression, perhaps the most concerning behavior, can originate from fear, territorial instincts, or previous negative experiences. To effectively address these behaviors, the first step is playing detective—observing when and where these behaviors occur can provide significant clues about their underlying causes.

Behavioral Modification Techniques

Once you've identified the root cause, the next step is employing humane behavioral modification techniques. Redirection, desensitization, and counterconditioning are invaluable tools in this endeavor. For instance, if your dog has a habit of chewing on inappropriate objects, redirection to suitable chew toys right when they start can gradually change their chewing preferences. It's like swapping out a toddler's crayon before they decorate your walls instead of paper. Desensitization involves gradually exposing your dog to the stimuli that trigger unwanted behaviors in a controlled manner, reducing their reaction over time. For example, if your dog barks at passersby, you might start by watching people from a distance, rewarding calm behavior, and gradually decreasing the distance.

Counterconditioning is particularly effective for addressing aggression. This technique involves changing your dog's emotional response to the stimuli that trigger aggression. If your dog reacts aggressively to other dogs, you could begin by associating the sight of other dogs at a distance with something positive, like their favorite treats or a fun game. Over time, they learn to associate other dogs with positive outcomes rather than as threats, effectively rewriting their emotional responses.

Role of Exercise in Behavior Management

Never underestimate the power of a good workout. Adequate physical and mental exercise can work wonders in alleviating many behavioral issues. Regular exercise helps burn off excess energy that might otherwise fuel destructive behaviors like chewing or hyperactivity. It also helps mitigate anxiety and stress, which are common culprits behind many behavioral problems. Incorporating activities that stimulate both their body and mind can help keep your dog balanced and happy. Think of it as a daily routine where you not only keep their body fit but their mind sharp and content. Activities like long walks, fetch, agility training, or even interactive playtimes with puzzle toys can significantly contribute to their overall behavioral health.

When to Seek Professional Help

While many behavioral issues can be managed with diligent training and modifications at home, there are times when professional help is needed. Recognizing these signs is crucial for the well-being of both you and your dog. If your dog shows persistent aggression, self-injurious behavior, or severe anxiety that does not improve despite your best efforts, it's time to call in the experts.

Professional dog trainers, behaviorists, or veterinarians can offer insights and interventions that are beyond the scope of home training. They can assess the situation objectively and provide targeted strategies that address the specific needs of your dog, ensuring their path to behavioral improvement is both safe and effective.

Navigating the complexities of dog behavior is much like learning a new dance. It takes two to tango, and both you and your dog have steps to learn. With patience, understanding, and the proper techniques, most behavioral issues can be effectively managed, leading to a harmonious living situation and a deeper bond between you and your canine companion. Just remember, every dog has its unique personality and quirks, and part of the joy of dog ownership is embracing and working through these challenges together.

TRAINING TIPS FOR SERVICE AND WORKING DOGS

Imagine you're embarking on a journey where your furry companion isn't just a pet but a crucial helper, a guide through the intricacies of daily life, or even a guardian in challenging work environments. Training service and working dogs is a venture that goes beyond basic obedience, diving deep into specialized skills that can significantly improve the lives of their handlers. These dogs aren't just learning to sit or stay; they are mastering tasks like guiding the visually impaired across busy streets, alerting a deaf person to a doorbell, or performing search and rescue missions. Each of these roles requires a tailored training approach that focuses intensely on reliability, precision, and adaptability.

Let's peel back the curtain on what makes training these remarkable dogs so unique. Unlike typical pet training, service and working dogs must achieve a level of obedience that's practically second nature. This kind of training starts with foundational obedience but quickly incorporates advanced skills specific to their future roles. For example, a guide dog for the blind must learn to navigate various obstacles while maintaining a direct and safe path for their handler. This includes stopping at curbs, avoiding low-hanging branches, and even disobeying a command if it would put the handler in danger, a concept known as intelligent disobedience.

Transitioning to task-specific training, each type of service dog has a different set of skills to master. Dogs trained for hearing assistance must learn to distinguish between everyday sounds and those that require a response, such as alarms or knocking. They must then alert their handler and lead them to the source of the sound. Similarly, psychiatric service dogs are trained to recognize signs of anxiety or distress in their handlers and perform tasks that alleviate or prevent escalation, such as providing tactile stimulation to help ground the person during a panic attack.

In the realm of legal and social considerations, navigating public spaces with a service dog comes with its set of challenges and rights. Understanding the legal definitions and rights concerning service dogs is crucial for handlers. Laws such as the Americans with Disabilities Act (ADA) in the United States provide the right of access to public places for service dogs and their handlers, ensuring that they are not denied entry or treated differently because of the presence of a service animal. However, these rights also come with responsibilities, such as ensuring the dog is well-behaved and does not pose a threat to public safety.

Support and resources for handlers of service and working dogs are vast, ranging from specialized training schools to online communities where handlers share advice and support. Training schools offer structured programs and experienced trainers who understand the nuances of service dog training. These schools often provide post-graduation support, helping handlers and their dogs adjust to their new working relationship. Online communities and forums can also be invaluable, offering a platform for handlers to connect, share experiences, and find solutions to common challenges.

Training a service or working dog is a profound responsibility that involves a deep understanding of the dog's role and the specific needs of the handler. It's about creating a partnership where both handler and dog understand and trust each other implicitly, achieving a level of communication and responsiveness that truly enhances the quality of life. Whether these dogs are opening doors, both literally and figuratively, or providing a sense of security in challenging environments, their training is about harnessing their natural abilities and shaping them into skills that can change lives.

THE IMPORTANCE OF CONSISTENCY AND PATIENCE IN DOG TRAINING

In the world of dog training, consistency is not just a practice; it's the golden thread that ties all your efforts together, creating a tapestry of trust and mutual understanding. Imagine you're trying to learn a new skill, like baking. If the instructions were to change every time you opened the recipe book, chances are, you'd end up with a batch of inedible cookies! Similarly, when training your dog, being consistent means using the same commands, rewards, and discipline each time. This consistency acts like a clear set of instructions that your dog can follow, understanding what is expected of them and what behaviors will earn them praise or a tasty treat.

Building this level of trust is crucial, especially in scenarios where your dog needs to follow commands for their safety, such as stopping at a busy street or coming when called away from a dangerous situation. Each time you're consistent, you reinforce their training, but more importantly, you reinforce their trust in you. They learn to associate your commands with specific outcomes, and this predictability makes it easier for them to respond appropriately, even in new or challenging situations. It's like having a reliable map on a journey; with it, your dog can navigate any path confidently.

Now, let's talk about patience, the unsung hero of dog training. Just as Rome wasn't built in a day, training your dog is a process that unfolds over time, with each day adding a brick to the foundation of their behavior. It's vital to recognize that progress can be slow and non-linear. Some days, you might feel like you're on a roll, and other days, it might seem like you're back to square one. This is perfectly normal. Dogs, like people, have good days and bad days. They can be affected by a variety of factors like their health, mood, and the environment.

During these training sessions, your patience is what makes the difference between a successful training outcome and a frustrated pup. If your dog is struggling to master a new command, instead of showing frustration, take a step back and break the command down into smaller, manageable parts. This not only makes it easier for your dog to learn but also keeps the training session positive and enjoyable for both of you. Remember, your dog is always looking to you for cues, and your calm, patient demeanor tells them that it's okay to make mistakes as long as they keep trying.

However, what about those inevitable setbacks? Maybe your dog mastered the 'sit' command, but suddenly, they're too distracted to follow through. When this happens, it's like hitting a pothole on a smooth road—it's jarring, but it's also an opportunity to fill the gap and smooth things over. Adjust your techniques, maybe by changing the training environment to one with fewer distractions or revisiting some of the earlier steps in the training process. The key is to maintain a calm and positive attitude. Your dog can sense your emotions, and if they pick up on your frustration, they might become anxious or reluctant to train, turning what should be a fun activity into a stressful ordeal.

Celebrating successes, no matter how small, is crucial. Did your dog finally sit on command after several attempts? Celebrate it! These celebrations reinforce their good behavior and make them eager to learn more. It's the same burst of joy you feel when someone appreciates your hard work—the motivation just skyrockets. Whether it's an extra treat, a cheerful praise, or a short play session, acknowledging your dog's efforts strengthens your bond and enhances the training experience.

Each training session is an investment in your dog's future, shaping them into a well-behaved and trusted companion. By being consistent and patient, you not only teach them commands, but you also teach them to trust, listen, and cooperate, qualities that define the enriching relationship you share with your furry friend. As you wrap up each session with a celebration of what you've both achieved, remember that training is not just about obedience; it's about growing together, learning from each other, and enjoying the journey, no matter how challenging it may be.

As we close this chapter on training, remember that the journey you're on with your dog is about more than just commands and obedience. It's about nurturing a relationship that is built on trust, respect, and mutual understanding. The lessons learned here set the stage for a lifetime of companionship and shared experiences. As we transition into the next chapter, we'll explore how to ensure your dog's health and wellness through proper care and attention to their physical needs, ensuring they remain by your side, healthy and happy, for years to come.

EXERCISE AND PHYSICAL ACTIVITY

Remember that time when you decided to start a new workout routine and enthusiastically jumped in, only to be sorely reminded the next day that perhaps you should have eased into it a bit more gently? Just like us, our dogs need the right amount and type of exercise tailored to their specific needs, which can vary tremendously based on factors like breed, age, and health. It's not just about keeping them physically fit; it's about enhancing their quality of life and avoiding the doggy equivalent of being unable to climb stairs after leg day.

ASSESSING YOUR DOG'S EXERCISE NEEDS BASED ON BREED AND AGE

Understanding Breed-specific Exercise Requirements

Let's dive into the world of breed-specific exercise needs. Picture two dogs: a Border Collie and a Bulldog. One, an epitome of canine athleticism, likely needs a good run over the hills just to start feeling warmed up. The other? Well, let's just say a few laps around the living room might suffice. Border Collies, renowned for their agility and stamina, were bred for herding sheep over vast, challenging terrains. They possess an almost bottomless well of energy and require significant physical activity not just to keep fit but to satisfy their mental need for stimulation. Without enough exercise, they might just decide your house is an excellent setting for an impromptu sheep herding trial.

On the flip side, Bulldogs are the lounge enthusiasts of the dog world, famous not just for their adorable squished faces but also for their laid-back attitude towards life. Their exercise needs are much less demanding, focusing on maintaining health rather than burning off excess energy. This doesn't mean they should be couch potatoes —regular, moderate exercise is crucial to keep them healthy, but compared to a Border Collie, they're more about quality over quantity.

Age-appropriate Exercise Plans

Just like humans, dogs' exercise needs change as they age. Puppies are like toddlers, brimming with energy and curiosity. Short, frequent play sessions throughout the day will help them burn off that puppy energy and keep them from redecorating your home with a toothy touch. As they grow into adulthood, their exercise needs increase, reaching a peak where they can handle more intensive activities like hiking or advanced agility training.

However, as dogs enter their senior years, their stamina starts to wane, and their exercise regime needs adjusting. Think of it as transitioning from full marathon training to a more leisurely morning walk. Senior dogs benefit immensely from regular, gentle exercise that keeps them mobile without straining their aging bodies.

Activities like slow-paced walks or light fetch games can keep them active while respecting their older bones and joints.

Assessing Individual Health Conditions

When planning your dog's exercise routine, it's crucial to consider any health issues that may impact the type and amount of physical activity they can safely handle. Conditions like heart disease, arthritis, or even past injuries can require modifications to their exercise regimen. For instance, a dog with heart disease might benefit from multiple short walks throughout the day rather than extended play sessions. This keeps them active without putting undue stress on their heart.

Consultation with Veterinarians

This is where regular vet visits come into play. A veterinarian can provide invaluable guidance tailored specifically to your dog's health needs. They can help you craft an exercise plan that maximizes benefits while minimizing risks, especially for puppies whose growing bodies are vulnerable or for seniors who might have hidden health issues. It's a bit like having a personal trainer who knows every ache and pain, as well as every burst of energy your dog has to offer.

Imagine you're planning a workout regimen for yourself with specific health constraints. You wouldn't just wing it, right? You'd likely consult with a professional and maybe get a tailored plan that fits just right. That's exactly what your vet does for your dog. This professional guidance ensures that your furry friend gets all the benefits of exercise without any of the downsides, keeping them bounding happily by your side for years to come.

OUTDOOR ACTIVITIES AND SPORTS FOR DOGS

Have you ever watched a dog at play in a wide-open space, ears flopping, tail wagging, and that unmistakable grin spread across their face? There's something utterly contagious about their sheer joy. It's this spirit of fun that makes engaging in outdoor activities and dog sports such a fantastic choice for keeping your furry friend healthy and happy. Not only do these activities help in maintaining physical fitness, but they also add a layer of excitement and challenge to your dog's routine, breaking the monotony of daily walks.

Let's explore the vibrant world of dog sports first. Agility training, for instance, is like the canine equivalent of an obstacle course race. It involves a series of challenges, such as weaving through poles, jumping over hurdles, and sprinting through tunnels. Agility not only tests your dog's fitness but also enhances their listening skills and ability to follow commands quickly. It's a thrilling mental and physical workout that can significantly strengthen the bond between you and your dog. Then there's flyball, a relay race that combines a sprint with the thrill of catching tennis balls from a specially designed launcher. Imagine the excitement as teams of dogs race against the clock, leaping hurdles and sprinting back to their handlers — it's a spectator sport as much as it is a participant one!

Dock jumping is another exhilarating sport where dogs run down a dock and leap as far as they can into the water, competing for distance or height. It's perfect for water-loving breeds or any dog who enjoys a good splash. The beauty of these sports lies not just in the physical exercise they provide but also in the sheer fun they offer, ensuring your dog is engaged, energized, and eager to participate.

Shifting gears from the competitive to the every day, the benefits of regular outdoor activities cannot be overstressed. Activities like hiking, swimming, or even a simple game of fetch in the park play a crucial role in improving your dog's cardiovascular health, keeping their joints healthy, and even helping to manage weight. Moreover, these activities can significantly reduce anxiety and behavioral issues. Dogs, much like humans, can feel cooped up or restless with too much pent-up energy. Regular outdoor play sessions help to dissipate this energy positively, promoting a calmer, more relaxed demeanor at home.

Incorporating play into exercise is not just beneficial; it's also incredibly rewarding. Picture this: you're in the park, frisbee in hand with your dog eagerly anticipating the throw. The moment it flies, they're off, every muscle working in harmony, eyes on the prize. This simple game enhances your dog's reflexes, teaches them focus and patience, and provides a healthy workout. Plus, it's a lot of fun! Similarly, using balls for fetching games encourages running and jumping, promoting endurance and agility. These play sessions are essential as they make the exercise routine exciting and varied, keeping your dog both physically and mentally stimulated.

Lastly, the social benefits of engaging in community dog sports or group walks are immense. These activities offer a fantastic opportunity for socialization, not just for your dog but also for you. Participating in group activities can help shy dogs come out of their shells, teaching them to be confident around other dogs and people. For you, it's a chance to connect with fellow dog lovers, share tips and stories, and perhaps even learn a thing or two from more experienced pet owners. Plus, it's always more fun to have company while enjoying the great outdoors.

Whether it's weaving through an agility course, jumping into a lake, or chasing down a frisbee, outdoor activities and sports offer a world of benefits and loads of fun for you and your dog. By integrating these into your routine, you're not just ensuring a fit, healthy dog but also a joyful and vibrant companion who thrives on shared adventures and new challenges.

INDOOR EXERCISES FOR BAD WEATHER DAYS

Rainy days can feel like a pause button on your dog's daily dash around the park. But, hey, here's the silver lining—indoor days open up a whole new playroom of fun and games that keep those tails wagging. Let's turn your living room into a mini-gym where you and your furry friend can dodge the drizzles and still get in some good, heart-pumping fun. Ever tried a game of hide and seek with your dog? It's not only a blast, but it also sharpens their problem-solving skills. Start simple: while your dog stays in one room, hide somewhere obvious in another and call their name. Reward them with treats and cuddles when they find you. As they get better at the game, you can pick more challenging hiding spots, making them rely more on their sniffing skills, which is a great mental workout!

Then there's tug-of-war, a classic that's good for both physical and mental exercise. It's not just about pulling; it's about cooperation and understanding commands like 'take it' and 'let go'. These commands are crucial in managing the play's intensity and ensuring it remains a positive experience. Make sure you use a sturdy toy that's meant for tugging, something that won't break apart and become a choking hazard. As you play, keep an eye on their body language to ensure they're enjoying the game and not getting overly excited or aggressive.

If you're feeling particularly crafty, why not set up a simple obstacle course? Use chairs to weave through, cushions for jumping over, and blankets over tables to create tunnels. It's like setting up a playground for your dog where they can hop, skip, and jump their way through the course. This type of play not only keeps them physically active but also stimulates their minds as they figure out how to navigate the challenges. Plus, it's a fantastic way for you both to bond and build trust as you guide them through the course, cheering them on at every turn.

Using Treadmills and Other Equipment

On days when the weather outside is frightful, and the fire is so delightful, dog treadmills can be a real game-changer. Yes, you heard that right—treadmills for dogs! They offer a fantastic way to ensure your pooch gets their necessary exercise without having to brave the elements. However, like any equipment, it's crucial to introduce your dog to a treadmill properly to ensure they find the experience positive and stress-free.

Start by letting them get used to the sight and sound of a running treadmill. You can do this by running it at a low speed without asking them to get on. Reward them with treats and affection as they investigate this new, humming contraption. Once they seem comfortable around it, encourage them to step on it while it's still off, again using treats to make the experience positive. Gradually, you can start the treadmill on the lowest setting, standing in front of it, holding their leash, and coaxing them to walk towards you. It's crucial to keep these initial sessions short and sweet, gradually increasing the duration as they get more comfortable. Always keep an eye on them while they're on the treadmill to ensure they're safe and not showing signs of stress or discomfort.

Interactive Toys and Games

Interactive toys are like puzzles for your pup, challenging their brain as much as their brawn. Treat-dispensing toys, for instance, are a household favorite. They require your dog to figure out how to manipulate the toy to release a treat, providing not only physical activity but also cognitive stimulation. These toys come in various shapes and complexities, from simple balls that slowly release treats as they roll to more intricate puzzle boxes that challenge even the cleverest of canines. The beauty of these toys lies in their ability to adapt to your dog's level of skill, keeping them engaged and motivated to solve the puzzle.

Routine and Consistency

Maintaining a routine is crucial, even when the weather turns your outdoor plans upside down. Dogs thrive on consistency, and keeping a regular schedule for activities helps manage their energy levels and prevents the type of boredom that can lead to unwanted behaviors like excessive barking or chewing. Set aside the same time each day for indoor exercise, just as you would for your daily walks. This helps your dog understand that just because it's wet and grey outside doesn't mean the fun and games are on hold. It reassures them that the good times are not just dependent on perfect weather but are a regular, reliable part of their day.

By incorporating these indoor activities into your routine, you ensure that your dog stays active, engaged, and, above all, close to you, turning dreary days into an opportunity for growth and bonding. Whether it's navigating an obstacle course in your living room, figuring out a new toy, or trotting on a treadmill, there's no shortage of ways to keep those tails wagging indoors.

SAFETY TIPS FOR EXERCISING WITH YOUR DOG

Let's put on our safety caps, shall we? Exercising with your dog should be fun, but let's not forget that safety plays a crucial role in keeping it enjoyable and beneficial for both of you. Think of it as preparing for a road trip; you check the car, pack the essentials, and make sure the weather's good for driving. Similarly, prepping your dog for exercise, especially if it's going to be a bit more strenuous than a leisurely walk, starts with a quick but thorough health check. Before you unleash that pent-up energy, take a moment to look your dog over. Are they limping slightly from yesterday's romp at the park? Do they seem more sluggish than usual, perhaps not as eager to grab their leash and go? These could be subtle signs of discomfort or fatigue that might warrant a day off or a vet visit instead of an adventure outdoors.

Speaking of outdoors, let's talk weather. It's not just about whether it's sunny or might rain; temperature plays a significant role in how safe it is for your dog to exercise outside. On hot days, the pavement can turn into a stovetop under those blazing rays, scorching those tender paws that are used to softer, cooler grass. Always touch the pavement with your hand before letting your dog walk on it; if it's too hot for your hand, it's too hot for them. And let's not forget the sneaky danger of heatstroke, which can creep up during those enthusiastic ball-chasing sessions under the sun. On the flip side, winter brings its own challenges. Ice, snow and the bitter cold can make walks uncomfortable and even dangerous. Ice-melting chemicals can irritate your dog's paws, and those chilly winds can quickly lead to hypothermia, especially in smaller or short-haired breeds.

Now, whether it's a sunny romp or a brisk winter walk, keeping your dog hydrated is critical. You might wonder, "Well, how much water does a dog need?" It's not like they can just tell you when they're thirsty. A good rule of thumb is to provide access to fresh water before and after any exercise, and if you're going out for a long session or it's particularly warm, bring water along with you. There are plenty of dog-friendly water bottles that include a bowl for easy drinking on the go. And after a good workout, just like us, dogs need time to cool down and rest. This downtime is crucial, allowing their muscles to relax and preventing them from over-working themselves. It's tempting to keep throwing that stick when you're both having a blast but watch for signs that it might be time to wind down. Panting that seems excessive, slowing down, or even stopping to lie down are your dog's ways of saying, "Hey, I might need a break."

Choosing where to exercise is as important as preparing for it. That quiet park where everyone seems to know each other and their dogs is a fantastic choice, far from busy roads and free from the dangers of heavy traffic. It's also wise to steer clear of areas that might have hidden hazards. Think less about those mysterious, rustling bushes (which are probably just a squirrel convention) and more about real dangers like toxic plants, unsecured trash that might contain food or substances harmful to dogs, or uneven terrain that could lead to injuries. Ensuring the environment is safe for a romp or workout session can mean the difference between a day full of fun and a day ending with an unexpected vet visit.

By keeping these safety tips in mind, exercising with your dog remains not just an activity but a shared joy that's both safe and rewarding. It's about creating memories while caring for their well-being, ensuring many more days of happy, healthy frolicking.

THE LINK BETWEEN EXERCISE AND WEIGHT MANAGEMENT

Have you ever watched your dog zoom around the park, tongue lolling out, eyes bright with excitement, and thought, "Wow, I wish I had that much energy"? It turns out that regular physical activity is just as crucial for your canine companion's health as it is for yours, especially when it comes to managing their weight. Let's face it, a chubby pup might be cute, but excess weight can lead to a slew of health issues, from arthritis to diabetes. Think of exercise as your dog's daily dose of health insurance, ensuring they stay not just within a healthy weight range but also vibrant and vigorous.

Starting with the basics, exercise is a powerhouse when it comes to weight control. It burns calories, sure, but it also revs up your dog's metabolism, even after they've flopped down for a post-play nap. It's like turning up the heat in a cold room; it takes a bit to get warm, but once it's cozy, it stays that way for a while. For dogs that are already tipping the scales, increasing their exercise can help shed those extra pounds. For those in the fit category, it keeps them from becoming a statistic in the growing obesity problem among pets.

Now, customizing exercise according to weight goals is where things get interesting. If your furry friend needs to lose a few, you might kick up the intensity of their workouts. More jogging or brisk walking, perhaps some extra rounds of fetch. Think of it as shifting from a leisurely stroll in the park to a more purposeful march. It's about getting their heart rate up and those calories burning. On the other hand, if your dog is more about maintaining their athletic figure, the exercise might be more about consistency than intensity —regular walks, daily playtime, and the occasional adventure to keep things interesting.

Bringing diet into the mix, it's crucial to align your dog's eating habits with their exercise routine. This synergy is what keeps their body in balance. Say you've amped up the exercise because your vet pointed out your dog could stand to lose a few pounds. It's going to be counterproductive if they're scarfing down more calories than they're burning. This is where consulting with a vet or a pet dietitian can really make a difference. They can help you craft a meal plan that complements the uptick in activity, making sure your dog gets the right balance of nutrients to support their more active lifestyle without packing on the pounds.

Monitoring your dog's progress is the final but ongoing piece of the weight management puzzle. Regular weigh-ins, body condition scoring, and keeping an eye on their energy levels are all part of this. It's like checking the air in your tires; it doesn't take long, but it's critical for a smooth ride. Adjustments may be needed along the way—maybe a tweak in their diet or a change in their exercise regimen—to ensure that your dog remains on the right track to a healthy weight.

By understanding the pivotal role of exercise in weight control, tailoring workouts to meet specific goals, aligning diet with physical activity, and keeping a close eye on progress, you're setting your dog up for a lifetime of health and happiness. It's about creating a lifestyle that supports their well-being from the ground up, ensuring they remain fit, agile, and ready to leap into action at the squeak of their favorite toy.

As we wrap up this exploration of exercise and its crucial role in maintaining your dog's weight and overall health, remember that each step you take together, whether it's on a forest trail or around the block, is a step towards a longer, happier life together. What we've covered here is not just about keeping your dog fit; it's about enhancing the quality of the time you share, filled with energy, joy, and health. Up next, we'll dive into preventative health measures, ensuring that your furry friend stays not only active and fit but also well-protected against common health issues that can affect dogs. Let's keep those tails wagging in good health!

PREVENTATIVE HEALTH CARE

Imagine, if you will, your dog's health as a lush, vibrant garden. Just as a gardener tends to their plants, pruning the overgrowth, nourishing the soil, and warding off pests, so too must you cultivate a regimen of care that keeps your furry friend thriving. Preventative health care for your dog isn't just about avoiding illness; it's about promoting a flourishing life. It's about understanding the rhythm of their needs through each season of their life and ensuring they have everything they need to grow strong and healthy—just like that garden you're imagining.

DESIGNING A PREVENTATIVE HEALTH CARE SCHEDULE

Establishing Routine Vet Visits

Let's start with the cornerstone of any good healthcare regimen: regular check-ups. Just as you wouldn't dream of skipping your annual physical (okay, maybe you would, but you shouldn't!), the same principle applies to your dog. Regular veterinary visits are crucial, not just for keeping vaccinations up to date, but for catching any potential health issues before they bloom into serious problems. The frequency of these visits can depend largely on the stage of your dog's life. Puppies might see the vet several times in their first year for all those initial check-ups and vaccines. Adult dogs generally need an annual check-up, while senior dogs might need to see their vet more frequently, as issues tend to crop up more often in older age.

Think of each vet visit as a checkpoint in the lifelong marathon of your dog's health. These visits are your opportunity to consult with your vet about nutrition, exercise, and any odd behaviors or symptoms that you've noticed. It's like having a coach who helps you tweak your training regimen and strategies to ensure peak performance—or in this case, peak tail-wagging and fetch-playing prowess.

Seasonal Considerations for Health Care

As the seasons change, so do the needs of your garden—and your dog. In the warmer months, flea and tick prevention is crucial. These pesky parasites are not only a nuisance but can carry diseases that are harmful to both you and your pup. Your vet can help you choose the best preventative treatments, which are often applied monthly during these warmer seasons. As the weather coots, joint care becomes paramount, especially for older dogs. Cold weather can exacerbate arthritis and other joint issues, so consider incorporating joint supplements or anti-inflammatory medications, as recommended by your vet, to keep your dog moving comfortably.

Age-Specific Care Routines

From the playful days of puppyhood to the dignified pace of senior years, each phase of your dog's life requires a slightly different approach to care. Puppies, for instance, are like sponges; they absorb everything and grow rapidly. They benefit from diets rich in proteins and fats that support their development and from vaccinations that protect against common youthful illnesses. Adult dogs require a balanced approach to maintain their health and vigor—regular exercise, dental care, and ongoing weight management. As your dog ages, their metabolism slows, and their dietary needs change. Senior dogs may require more fiber, less fat, and more frequent veterinary visits to manage the natural aging process.

Keeping Record of Health Data

Imagine trying to remember every plant you've ever grown, when you watered them, and when you last fertilized—without a gardening journal. Similarly, keeping a health record for your dog helps you track vaccinations, vet visits, and any past health issues. This record is invaluable, not just for your regular vet but in case of emergencies or if you have to visit a new clinic. It ensures that any veterinarian can quickly understand your dog's medical history, making it easier to provide the best care possible.

Incorporating these preventative measures into your dog's care routine is akin to a gardener who knows exactly when to water, prune, or fertilize to keep their garden thriving. With careful planning and regular care, you can help ensure that your dog enjoys a healthy, happy life, season after season.

VACCINATIONS AND REGULAR HEALTH CHECKS

When you think about keeping your dog healthy, vaccinations are like the shield and armor in an epic battle against diseases. They're not just a formality but a crucial line of defense that protects your furry friend from various ailments that can severely affect their health—and in some cases, even prove fatal. Understanding the nuances between core and non-core vaccinations can help you tailor this shield to be as robust as it needs to be, depending on where you live and how your dog spends their days.

Core vaccinations are essentially the standard armor issued to all dogs. These include vaccines for rabies, distemper, parvovirus, and adenovirus. Think of these as non-negotiables—no matter where you live or what your dog's lifestyle is, these vaccinations are vital. They protect against diseases that are widespread, highly contagious, and often deadly. On the other hand, non-core vaccinations are more like customizable armor enhancements. These depend on your dog's exposure risk, which can vary based on factors like geographic location, lifestyle, and even the local climate. For example, the Lyme disease vaccine is recommended for dogs in areas where ticks are common, while the Bordetella vaccine is a good idea for those who frequent dog parks or boarding facilities.

Scheduling these vaccinations properly from puppyhood to adulthood is crucial and can be thought of as laying down a protective foundation, one layer at a time. Puppies typically start their vaccination series around six to eight weeks of age and continue with boosters every three to four weeks until they're about 16 weeks old. This series is crucial as it builds their initial immunity while their young bodies are still developing. As adults, dogs generally move to an annual vaccination schedule, although some vaccines might be administered every three years. It's important to discuss these details with your vet, as they can recommend a schedule that aligns best with your dog's specific needs and risks.

Now, let's walk through what happens during a regular veterinary health check, because it's about so much more than just updating vaccines. Picture this: you and your dog walk into the vet's office for a check-up. After some initial tail wags and perhaps a few treats, your vet will start with a thorough physical examination. They'll check your dog from nose to tail—listening to their heart and lungs, examining their teeth, feeling their abdomen, checking their skin and coat quality, and looking for any signs of unusual lumps or swelling. These exams are crucial not just for assessing overall health but for catching early signs of issues like heart disease, diabetes, or even cancer. Early detection can make a significant difference in treatment success and can often lead to better outcomes for your dog.

Educating yourself on how to monitor your dog's health at home is another layer of protection you can provide them. Regularly checking for signs of illness or discomfort can help you catch potential health issues before they become serious. Start by getting familiar with your dog's normal behavior, appetite, and energy levels. Any significant changes in these areas could be a red flag that something's up. Also, keep an eye on their stool and urine: changes in consistency, color, or frequency are often early indicators of health problems. Regularly feeling your dog's body for any new lumps, bumps, or tender areas can also help you catch issues like tumors or abscesses early, making treatments more manageable and less invasive.

By staying vigilant at home and keeping up with regular vet visits and vaccination schedules, you're doing everything in your power to ensure your dog leads a long, healthy life. It's a testament to the depth of your bond and the seriousness with which you take their well-being. Just like any good knight would do for their trusted steed, right?

THE IMPORTANCE OF DENTAL CARE IN DOGS

When it comes to your dog's health, their mouth is a lot more than just a vehicle for slobbery kisses; it's a gateway to their overall well-being. Think of dental health like the roots of a tree—largely out of sight but critical to the health of the entire organism. Neglecting those roots can lead to problems that affect far more than just the tree's appearance. In dogs, poor dental hygiene can lead to a slew of health issues, including heart and kidney diseases. This happens because bacteria from the mouth can enter the bloodstream and travel to various organs, setting up camp and causing infections or inflammation that can seriously impact your furry friend's health. It's a stealthy escalation that can often be nipped in the bud with regular dental care.

Now, let's talk about the nuts and bolts of keeping those doggy teeth sparkling. Daily tooth brushing might sound like overkill, but it's as beneficial for your dog as it is for you. Start with a dog-specific toothbrush and toothpaste—never use human toothpaste, as it can contain ingredients like xylitol, which is toxic to dogs. Introduce the toothbrush gradually, letting your dog sniff and lick it so they see it as a treat, not a threat. Then, gently lift the lips and brush in a circular motion, focusing on the gum line where plaque tends to accumulate. It's a bonding activity that, while potentially sloppy at first, can become a cherished part of your daily routine.

Chews and toys also play a crucial role in dental health. Not only do they help reduce plaque and tartar build-up, but they also satisfy your dog's natural chewing instinct, which can save your shoes and furniture from becoming casualties. Look for chews that are designed to be tough and durable, as well as those that have received a seal of approval from veterinary dental organizations. These products are often designed to provide mechanical cleaning of the teeth, akin to how dental floss works for us, scraping away the plaque as your dog chews.

Professional dental cleanings by a veterinarian are not just an upsell; they are a necessary procedure for maintaining your dog's health, especially as they age. During a professional cleaning, which usually requires anesthesia, your vet will remove plaque and tartar from above and below the gum line—a thoroughness that home brushing can't match. They'll also polish the teeth to smooth out any nooks where bacteria could gather, and they'll evaluate dental health, checking for signs of potential issues like gum disease or loose teeth. The frequency of these cleanings can vary depending on factors like your dog's age, breed, and overall dental health, but they typically should happen at least once a year.

To keep your dog's mouth in tip-top shape, consider integrating dental-friendly diets and treats into their routine. Some pet food manufacturers offer prescription dental diets that are specially formulated to reduce tartar build-up; these can be a great option, especially for dogs that are prone to dental issues. Water additives and sprays can also contribute to oral hygiene, offering an easy way to combat plaque continuously.

By prioritizing dental care, you're doing more than ensuring fresh breath and a beautiful smile; you're laying the foundation for a healthier, happier life for your canine companion. It's an investment in their health that pays dividends in cuddles, kisses, and years of companionship.

PREVENTING COMMON CANINE DISEASES

When you think of your dog, you likely envision a bundle of joy who's always ready to play fetch or curl up beside you. Yet, beneath their playful exterior, each dog carries a genetic blueprint that could predispose them to certain hereditary conditions. It's much like inheriting a family heirloom; some might bestow resilience and strength, while others might carry vulnerabilities. For instance, Dachshunds are famously prone to back issues, while Boxers have higher risks of heart conditions. This genetic lottery makes it crucial to consider genetic screening, especially if you're working with a breeder. Screening tests can provide a sneak peek into your dog's genetic makeup, offering valuable insights into what health issues they might face down the road. By understanding these risks early on, you can tailor your care to mitigate them, perhaps through specific diets, regular check-ups, or preventive surgeries.

Switching gears from genetics to lifestyle, let's talk about diseases that are often self-invited through lifestyle choices, such as obesity, diabetes, and heart disease. These conditions aren't just human woes; our dogs share these risks, particularly if their lifestyle involves more snoozing than moving or more treats than balanced meals. To combat these, integrating a proper diet and regular exercise into your dog's routine is vital. Think of it as setting a rhythm to their daily life that includes not just meals and naps but also playtimes and walks. For diet, lean meats, healthy fats, and fibrous vegetables can maintain their weight and support overall health. Combine this with daily walks or play sessions, and you help maintain their cardiovascular health, keep their joints agile, and manage their weight, all of which can stave off the creep of lifestyle-related diseases.

Environmental factors also play a significant role in your dog's health. Diseases like Lyme disease, which is transmitted by ticks, or leptospirosis, a bacterial disease that dogs can contract from water sources or soil, can pose serious health risks. Preventing these diseases involves a keen awareness of your environment and proactive measures. For tick prevention, regular use of tick control products and checking your dog's coat after walks in the woods or tall grasses are effective strategies. Vaccines are available for diseases like Lyme disease, offering another layer of protection. For leptospirosis, avoiding allowing your dog to drink from or swim in stagnant water or areas known for wildlife urine, which can contaminate natural water sources, is crucial. These steps are like setting up a security system; they help keep the invaders out, ensuring your dog's environment supports their health, not threatens it.

Regular screening tests are the watchdogs of your dog's health regimen. They can sniff out issues long before they become visible. Blood tests, for example, are fantastic at uncovering early signs of kidney or liver disease, while X-rays can spot the first signs of hip dysplasia or other skeletal issues. These tests should be a regular part of your dog's health care, much like routine maintenance checks are for a car. They allow you to catch potentially serious health issues early, often making the difference between a manageable condition and a severe health crisis. Regular screenings empower you with knowledge, and in the realm of health, knowledge is not just power—it's prevention, it's peace of mind, and, in many cases, it's the promise of more happy years with your furry best friend.

Incorporating these preventive measures into your care routine sets a standard of health that acts like a shield against common canine diseases. It's about being proactive rather than reactive, about setting up defenses, and about creating a lifestyle that prioritizes wellness. With these strategies in play, you're not just protecting your dog from illnesses but actively enhancing the quality and longevity of their life. They rely on you, after all, to not just love them but to lead them in a dance of health that keeps them twirling happily at your side, year after joyful year.

TITER TESTING AS A VACCINATION ALTERNATIVE

Imagine you're back in your school science class, and today's lesson is about vaccinations and immune response. Instead of a pop quiz, however, the subject is your beloved pup and how to ensure they're protected without over-vaccination. This is where titer testing, an often-overlooked tool in canine health, comes into play. Think of titer tests as a report card showing how well your dog's immune system has responded to previous vaccinations. Specifically, these tests measure the levels of antibodies in your dog's bloodstream, which are proteins produced in response to antigens (virus particles in vaccines). If the antibody levels are high enough, your dog is considered protected against the diseases for which they were vaccinated.

The beauty of titer testing lies in its ability to reduce the frequency of vaccinations without compromising your dog's health. It's like having a window into your dog's immune system, allowing you to make informed decisions about whether they truly need another vaccine. This can be particularly advantageous for adult or senior dogs whose immune systems have responded to years of vaccinations. By using titer tests, you can avoid unnecessary vaccinations, which not only spares your dog from potential side effects but also reduces the overall stress and discomfort associated with the vaccination process.

Interpreting titer results can seem daunting, but it's mostly about understanding the numbers. A positive titer does not mean your dog is immune to disease but rather that their immune system has responded to a particular vaccine at a level that is typically protective. Conversely, a negative titer suggests that your dog may not have sufficient immunity and might need a booster vaccine. However, it's crucial to consult with your veterinarian to interpret these results within the context of your dog's overall health and lifestyle, as well as regional disease risks.

Integrating titer testing into your dog's regular healthcare regimen is a proactive approach that aligns with responsible vaccination practices. It begins with a discussion with your veterinarian, ideally during one of your regular health checks. You can plan for titer testing to coincide with your dog's annual check-up, making it part of a holistic health assessment. If the titer results indicate that your dog is still protected, you can skip the corresponding vaccine for that cycle, which not only saves you from unnecessary expenses but also aligns with a more tailored approach to your dog's health care. This personalized strategy ensures that each aspect of your dog's healthcare routine is specifically calibrated to meet their unique needs.

By adopting titer testing, you're embracing a nuanced view of vaccination—one that respects the science of immunology and acknowledges the individual needs of your dog. This method not only maintains their health but also deepens your understanding of how best to protect and care for your furry companion. It's a sophisticated approach that goes beyond the one-size-fits-all vaccination schedule, offering a pathway that is as informed as it is compassionate.

As we wrap up this chapter on preventative health care, we've explored everything from routine check-ups to the nuanced use of titer testing. Each section has been a step towards understanding how best to keep your dog healthy from puppyhood through their golden years. These proactive measures aren't just tasks on a checklist; they're expressions of love and commitment to your furry family member's well-being. As we turn the page, we'll delve into the next chapter where we explore the world of canine mental health, ensuring your dog's emotional needs are just as nurtured as their physical ones. Here's to a life of health and happiness for your pup, guided by thoughtful care every step of the way.

HOLISTIC HEALTH AND ALTERNATIVE THERAPIES

L et's face it, when you first hear "holistic health," you might picture someone whispering affirmations to plants or meditating beside a stack of crystals. But when it comes to the health of our furry companions, holistic practices go beyond these stereotypes, diving deep into an approach that treats the whole dog—mind, body, and spirit—rather than just chasing after symptoms as they pop up like an annoying game of whack-a-mole. It's about creating a balance that supports overall well-being, ensuring our dogs aren't just living, but thriving.

HOLISTIC HEALTH CARE: TREATING MORE THAN JUST SYMPTOMS

Holistic health care for dogs, much like in humans, revolves around a philosophy that views the body as an interconnected system. This approach seeks to maintain health through balance and prevention rather than merely reacting to illness. Think of it as regular maintenance on your car; you wouldn't wait for it to break down before changing the oil, right? Similarly, holistic health practices in dogs might include nutrition plans tailored to their specific needs, herbal supplements, regular physical therapy, and stress-reducing techniques—all aimed at preventing issues rather than treating them only after they arise.

This proactive approach ensures that we're not just putting out fires but are building a fire-resistant structure. It's about nurturing an environment where potential health issues have a harder time taking root, much like preparing your garden soil with everything it needs so pests and weeds (read: diseases) have less chance to thrive.

Exploring the Spectrum of Holistic Modalities

When diving into the world of holistic modalities, the variety can be as vast and varied as dog breeds themselves. Each modality offers unique benefits, and understanding how they contribute to your dog's health can be quite an adventure.

- **Homeopathy**: This method is based on "like cures like." Tiny, highly diluted doses of natural substances are used to help the body heal itself. It's akin to using a pinch of pepper to stop a sneeze—it might sound counterintuitive, but it can work wonders.
- **Naturopathy**: This involves using natural remedies such as herbs, massage, and physical therapy, focusing on supporting the natural healing processes of the body. If homeopathy is like fine-tuning your dog's internal engine, naturopathy is about giving it the right fuel and regular tune-ups.
- **Chiropractic Care**: Yes, dogs can benefit from chiropractic adjustments too! This practice focuses on the manipulation of the spine to ensure optimal alignment,

which can help the nervous system function at its best. Think of it as keeping the communication lines open and clear, ensuring every part of the body gets the memo on how to stay healthy.

Integrating Holistic Practices with Conventional Veterinary Care

Marrying holistic practices with traditional veterinary medicine can give your dog the best of both worlds. It's like having both a belt and suspenders—extra secure. For instance, while your vet might prescribe medication to treat a symptom, integrating a holistic approach could involve adjusting your dog's diet to help mitigate the side effects of the medication or prevent the recurrence of the issue. It's about creating a tailored suit of health care that fits your dog perfectly.

Consider a scenario where your dog suffers from arthritis. Traditional medicine might provide anti-inflammatory medications to ease the pain, which is great for immediate relief. Holistically, you might add in a regimen of physical therapy to help strengthen the muscles around the joints and improve flexibility, reducing the overall strain on the joints and potentially decreasing the dependence on medications.

Evaluating Effectiveness and Safety

Now, while the holistic approach offers many benefits, it's important to navigate these waters with a map and compass. Not all practices are created equal, and what works for one dog might not work for another. Consulting with a veterinarian who has experience in holistic medicine can provide you with a balanced perspective. They can help you weigh the benefits against any risks and tailor a holistic plan that complements your dog's conventional treatments.

When evaluating different holistic options, consider factors like the credentials of the practitioner, the quality of the supplements, and the specific needs of your dog. It's a bit like choosing a new vet or a doggy daycare—you want to ensure that they have your dog's best interests at heart and that they're qualified to provide the care your dog needs.

Navigating the realm of holistic health care for your dog is a journey of love, patience, and sometimes, a bit of trial and error. But when you see your dog running through the fields, their coat shiny, their eyes bright, and their tail wagging like a metronome set to a lively tempo, you'll know that every step on this holistic path has been worth it. Remember, the goal isn't just to treat a sick dog but to foster an environment where they can achieve optimal health and happiness naturally.

THE USE OF ACUPUNCTURE IN CANINE HEALTH

Imagine for a moment your dog could tell you about that nagging back pain or that tweak in the knee after an exuberant leap for a frisbee. Well, while they can't speak, there's a time-honored method from traditional Chinese medicine that might just do the speaking for them: acupuncture. Coming from a practice that has treated countless ailments in humans for over 2,000 years, acupuncture for dogs works under the same principles. It's all about restoring balance and enhancing the body's natural healing processes. The core idea here revolves around Qi (pronounced "chee"), which is considered the vital life energy flowing through the body. When Qi flows freely, your dog is in a state of good health. However, if this flow is blocked or unbalanced, it can lead to disease or discomfort.

By inserting ultra-thin needles into specific points along the body, an acupuncturist aims to clear these blockages and stimulate the body's natural healing abilities. It's akin to tuning a musical instrument to ensure each note resonates perfectly.

Now, you might be wondering what sort of conditions in dogs might benefit from such a practice. Well, acupuncture has a pretty impressive repertoire. It is frequently used to treat chronic pain conditions such as arthritis, which can significantly affect a dog's quality of life as they age. But that's not all; it's also effective for nerve injuries, helping to restore mobility and reduce pain in conditions that might otherwise require extensive medication. Additionally, certain types of gastrointestinal issues and even some dermatological problems can see improvement from acupuncture. This method can be a game-changer, especially for managing symptoms in chronic conditions where conventional treatments might fall short or cause undesirable side effects.

When you walk into a typical acupuncture session for your dog, it's quite a serene experience, far removed from the clinical atmosphere of a regular vet visit. Sessions usually last between 30 to 60 minutes, and the number of needles used can vary depending on the condition being treated. The acupuncturist will gently insert needles into specific points on your dog's body, which, surprisingly, most dogs tolerate very well. In fact, it's not uncommon for our furry friends to become so relaxed they drift off to sleep during the session. The needles are typically left in place for about 15 to 30 minutes, during which time your dog can rest comfortably, often showing signs of relaxation and ease.

Finding a qualified practitioner, however, is where you need to channel your inner detective skills. This isn't about just finding someone who's good with dogs and needles but a licensed veterinary acupuncturist whose training specifically includes acupuncture alongside a foundational veterinary practice. The International Veterinary Acupuncture Society is a great place to start, offering resources and links to certified practitioners. Ensuring the practitioner has the right credentials is crucial because, just as with human acupuncture, the precision and understanding of the points and the flow of Qi require significant training and knowledge. A well-trained veterinary acupuncturist will not only provide effective treatment but will also understand when acupuncture might not be the best option, integrating it with conventional treatments to achieve the best outcomes for your dog's health.

As you explore this ancient yet innovative treatment option, remember that each dog, like each human, is unique in how they respond to different therapies. Acupuncture might be the missing piece of the puzzle in managing your dog's health issues, offering a gentle, effective way to enhance their well-being and vitality. Whether it's helping your elderly pooch find relief from joint pain or aiding in the recovery from a nerve injury, the art of acupuncture is about opening doors to new possibilities in canine health care, providing a fusion of age-old wisdom and modern veterinary understanding.

BENEFITS OF HERBAL SUPPLEMENTS FOR DOGS

Imagine you're in your garden, plucking herbs not just for your dinner but also to boost your furry friend's health. It sounds a bit like a modern-day witchcraft, but it's actually about tapping into the age-old wisdom of herbal supplements that can benefit your dog. Picture turmeric, not just spicing up your curry but easing your pup's inflammation; ginger, not only jazzing up your tea but also soothing your dog's digestion; and milk thistle, protecting not just medieval liver ailments but also your modern dog's liver from toxins. These herbs have been used by humans for centuries and, when used correctly, can be just as beneficial for our canine companions.

Let's start with turmeric, a vibrant yellow spice that's as good at reducing inflammation as it is at staining your countertops. It contains a compound called curcumin, which has been widely praised for its anti-inflammatory properties. For dogs suffering from arthritis or other inflammatory conditions, incorporating turmeric into their diet can help reduce pain and improve mobility. It's like turning back the clock on your dog's joints, allowing them to romp around with the youthful vigor of a puppy.

Next up, ginger, which is renowned for its stomach-soothing quali-ties. If your dog ever suffers from nausea or bloat, a little ginger can go a long way. It works by helping to relax the muscles in the gut and speed up the digestion process, which can help to alleviate discomfort and settle their stomach. Think of it as a gentle pat on your dog's back, easing their digestive woes and helping them to feel more comfortable after meals.

Milk thistle is another herb with a powerhouse of benefits, particu-larly known for its liver-protecting properties. It acts almost like a shield, protecting the liver from toxins and helping to regenerate liver cells. If your dog is on medication that may be hard on their liver, or if they're recovering from a liver-related illness, milk thistle can be a supportive supplement in their diet. It's like giving their liver an extra layer of armor, bolstering its defenses against the slings and arrows of outrageous fortune—or just everyday toxins.

Now, while the benefits of these herbs can be impressive, it's crucial to use them safely. Herbs are powerful, and just like any medicine, they need to be used in the right doses and with an understanding of potential side effects. For instance, too much turmeric can cause stomach upset or even lead to kidney stones if used excessively. Ginger, while mostly safe, can act as a blood thinner, which might be a concern if your dog is on similar medication. And milk thistle, though beneficial, can interact with certain drugs by affecting how they are metabolized in the liver.

Ensuring you're using the correct dosages and being aware of potential interactions with other medications your dog might be taking is vital. It's always best to consult with a veterinarian, ideally one with experience in herbal medicine, before adding these to your dog's regimen. They can help you understand the appropriate dosages and any potential interactions, ensuring that the herbs provide their benefits without unintended side effects.

Incorporating these herbs into your dog's diet can be as simple as adding a sprinkle of powdered turmeric to their meal, mixing a bit of ginger into their kibble, or using a milk thistle supplement as directed by your vet. These additions can make mealtime not just a routine but a ritual, one that imbues your dog's food with both flavor and medicinal benefits. It transforms their bowl into a cauldron of healthful brew, where each ingredient contributes to their vitality and well-being.

Embracing the use of herbal supplements in your dog's health regimen opens up a world of natural remedies that can support and enhance their well-being in conjunction with conventional treatments. It's about blending the best of what nature and science have to offer, ensuring your dog can enjoy a happy, healthy life by your side. Whether it's the anti-inflammatory properties of turmeric, the digestive support of ginger, or the liver-protecting power of milk thistle, these herbs provide a spectrum of benefits that can help address some of the common health issues faced by dogs today.

MASSAGE AND PHYSICAL THERAPY TECHNIQUES

Imagine a scenario where you come home from a long day, your muscles aching and your joints whining with each step. Now, picture someone giving you a soothing massage or guiding you through a gentle stretching routine. Feels heavenly, right? Our canine companions, much like us, can also reap enormous benefits from the art of massage and physical therapy. These practices are not just about pampering; they're a cornerstone of holistic health that can dramatically improve your dog's life, especially if they're recovering from an injury or managing chronic issues like arthritis.

Massage therapy for dogs functions similarly to human massage by enhancing circulation, relieving muscle tension, and promoting a deep sense of relaxation. It's particularly beneficial for active dogs or those in their golden years. Increased circulation means that blood, rich in oxygen and nutrients, flows more effectively to tired or injured tissues, promoting faster healing and reducing inflammation. For an older dog, this can mean a lot. It can transform their slow, stiff walk into a more fluid motion, making their daily stroll around the block more enjoyable rather than a painful task. It's like oiling a rusty hinge so that it moves smoothly without a squeak.

Now, let's get hands-on with some basic massage techniques you can try at home. First, create a calm environment; maybe put on some soft music and ensure a comfortable surface for your dog to lie on. Start with gentle petting to help them relax. Once they seem calm, begin with long, slow strokes down their body. Watch their reaction to ensure they're comfortable. You can then progress to a more structured massage, using the heels of your palms to gently apply pressure along their muscles, particularly along the spine, but avoiding direct pressure on the bones. Focus on areas where their muscles are more pronounced, and you might feel tension. The key is to keep your movements fluid and gentle. If at any point they seem uncomfortable, ease up. It's all about listening to their body.

Physical therapy, on the other hand, is more about movement and less about stillness. It's designed to enhance mobility and strength through specific exercises that you can do at home. For instance, if your dog is recovering from knee surgery, simple exercises like assisted standing or slow, controlled walks can significantly aid their recovery. You can also use techniques like passive range-of-motion exercises, where you gently move their joints through their normal range of movement to improve joint health and flexibility. It's similar to helping a friend stretch before a run, only here, you're helping your dog maintain or regain their mobility.

When it comes to professional services, knowing when and how to seek them can make a significant difference in your dog's health outcomes. While basic massage and simple physical therapy exercises can be safely performed at home, more severe conditions or post-operative recoveries often require professional intervention. Professionals bring a level of expertise that ensures techniques such as deep tissue massage or therapeutic ultrasound are done correctly, maximizing benefits while minimizing risks.

Finding the right professional involves looking for qualifications such as certification in canine massage or physical therapy from recognized institutions. Many vets offer these services, or they can refer you to a trusted professional. It's similar to finding a good doctor; you want someone knowledgeable, experienced, and, importantly, someone your dog feels comfortable with. These professionals not only provide hands-on treatment but can also teach you techniques to use at home, making you a proactive participant in your dog's health care routine.

Exploring the world of massage and physical therapy offers a deeper dive into managing your dog's health in a hands-on, interactive way. It's about more than just easing pain; it's about enhancing life quality, strengthening your bond through touch, and actively participating in their physical health maintenance. Whether through your gentle strokes or the skilled hands of a professional, these therapies can open up a world of comfort and mobility for your dog, making every movement a joy rather than a challenge.

INTEGRATING CBD OIL INTO YOUR DOG'S HEALTH REGIMEN

Now, let's cozy up and chat about something you've probably heard buzzing around the dog park lately: CBD oil. Yes, that CBD, derived from the cannabis plant but without the 'high' that comes with THC. It's like decaf coffee—keeping the good without the buzz. In the canine world, CBD is gaining fans faster than a dropped hot dog, thanks to its potential health benefits. These range from reducing anxiety and inflammation to managing pain and possibly even more. Let's unwrap this package together, shall we?

Picture CBD oil as a versatile tool in your dog-care toolkit. Extracted mainly from the hemp variety of cannabis, which has low THC levels, CBD oil is like a Swiss Army knife for health issues. It works by interacting with the endocannabinoid system, which most creatures, including our furry friends, naturally possess. This system plays a crucial role in maintaining balance in the body, and when CBD is introduced, it can help regulate and stabilize various functions. Think of it as helping your dog's internal orchestra stay in tune, ensuring each section plays in harmony, from nerves to digestion to immune responses.

But before you jump on the bandwagon and start drizzling CBD oil over your dog's kibble, there are a few chords we need to strike, particularly regarding legality and quality. The legal status of CBD can be a bit like a patchwork quilt, varying significantly from one place to another. In some areas, it's perfectly legal, while in others, it may still be under tight restrictions. It's crucial to play detective and research the laws in your region to ensure you're on the right side of the law. After all, no one wants a simple quest for pet health to end in a legal mishap.

Once you've got the green light legally, the next step is finding high-quality, vet-approved CBD products. This market can be a Wild West of sorts, with products ranging from the good, the bad, to the ugly. Look for products specifically formulated for pets, and always check for third-party testing. These tests should confirm the CBD content and verify the product is free from contaminants like pesticides and heavy metals. Think of it as checking the nutritional label on your cereal box; you want to know it's packed with good stuff and free from anything that could cause harm.

Now, let's talk about getting down to business—dosage and administration. This part is crucial because even the best tool, when used incorrectly, can turn a solution into a new problem. Starting with a low dose and gradually increasing is a standard approach. Typically, dosages are calculated based on weight, but just like diets, one size doesn't fit all. It's more art than science, requiring careful observation and adjustments. Administration can be as simple as mixing the oil in your dog's food or using a dropper to administer it directly into their mouth. Whichever route you choose, the goal is consistent and controlled administration, keeping an eye out for how they react to the oil.

Monitoring and adjusting the treatment is where your keen observation skills come into play. Just like tuning an instrument, you listen for the sounds of improvement or any signs of discord. Improvement can manifest as more pep in their step, less anxiety during thunderstorms, or perhaps a more relaxed demeanor overall. If you notice adverse effects, which might include lethargy or digestive upset, it's important to adjust the dosage or consult with your vet. Keeping a log can be helpful, jotting down what you administer and how your dog responds, turning your observations into valuable data that can help tailor the treatment to your dog's specific needs.

Navigating the world of CBD for your dog is a journey of care, observation, and continuous learning. It's about enhancing their quality of life, armed with the correct information, the best products, and a clear understanding of how to use them effectively. As you integrate CBD oil into your dog's health regimen, you're taking steps not just toward alleviating symptoms but potentially opening the door to a happier, healthier life for your furry best friend.

As we wrap up this exploration into holistic health and alternative therapies, remember that each step you take—from choosing acupuncture to integrating CBD oil—is about more than just treatments. It's about building a deeper understanding of your dog's health needs and strengthening the bond you share through attentive, informed care. Next, we'll venture into the world of behavioral training, where understanding and communication meet action, to further enrich the lives of our beloved canine companions.

BEHAVIORAL AND MENTAL WELLNESS

Imagine you've just settled in for a cozy evening; perhaps you're curled up with a good book or about to start a movie marathon, and your faithful furry friend is right there beside you—only, instead of relaxing, they seem on edge. Every creak of the house, every gust of wind seems to send a shiver down their spine. It's like watching a mystery thriller where you're both on the edge of your seats, but only one of you is enjoying the suspense. Understanding and managing your dog's anxiety and stress is crucial, not just for their well-being but for yours too. After all, a calm dog means a calm house, and who doesn't want that?

UNDERSTANDING CANINE ANXIETY AND STRESS TRIGGERS

Let's dive into the world of canine anxiety and stress. Much like humans, dogs can feel overwhelmed by the hustle and bustle of daily life or changes in their routines and environment. Common triggers include loud noises like thunderstorms or fireworks that can send them scampering for cover under the nearest bed. Separation anxiety is another biggie; it can manifest when you leave for work, turning your departure into a scene worthy of an opera—full of dramatic howls and heart-wrenching whimpers. Then there are the less obvious but equally impactful changes in the environment, such as moving to a new home or even rearranging furniture, which can disturb their sense of security and territory.

Now, spotting these stress signals in your dog can be as tricky as solving a whodunit. Physiological signs often include excessive panting that isn't heat-related, shaking or trembling, and avoidance behaviors like hiding or escaping. They might also show changes in bodily functions, like having accidents indoors despite being house-trained. These signs are your dog's way of waving a big red flag that something's up. By being observant, you can start to piece together what's triggering their anxiety and address it head-on.

The emotional toll of constant stress on dogs can be substantial. Just like a stress-filled lifestyle can make us humans cranky or with-drawn, prolonged stress can lead to behavioral changes in dogs, such as increased aggression towards people or other animals or an unusually withdrawn and subdued temperament. These signs aren't just your dog having a bad day—they're indications of a deeper issue that needs addressing.

Fortunately, there are strategies to help manage and prevent these anxiety triggers. Establishing a routine can work wonders; it creates a predictable environment that reduces anxiety because your dog knows what to expect and when. Think of it as setting a daily schedule that includes regular meal times, walks, and quiet time—it can help them feel more secure and less anxious. Predictability is comforting to dogs, much like a favorite comfort movie is to us; they know the plot and that there are no surprises. Early exposure to various stimuli can also enhance their adaptability, making them less likely to react negatively to changes in their surroundings or routines. Think of it as social training—they get to meet and greet different scenarios in a controlled way, which can help reduce their stress levels in future encounters.

Visual Element: Chart of Stress Signs in Dogs

To help you better understand and recognize signs of stress in your dog, here's a simple chart that outlines key physiological and behavioral signs of stress. This visual guide can serve as a quick reference when you're trying to figure out if your dog is just being quirky or if they're actually showing signs of anxiety or stress.

- **Panting:** Look for excessive panting that isn't related to heat or physical exertion.
- **Shaking/Trembling:** Notice if your dog shakes or trembles in situations where they are not cold.
- **Avoidance:** Watch for behaviors like hiding or attempting to escape, which can indicate fear or discomfort.
- **Accidents:** Observe any uncharacteristic house soiling which could be a sign of distress.
- **Behavior Changes:** Be aware of any sudden aggression or withdrawal, as these can be emotional responses to stress.

This chart serves as a starting point for you to become more attuned to your dog's emotional and physical state, enabling you to provide better support and intervention when they need it most. By keeping an eye on these signs and acting on them, you can help ensure your dog's mental and emotional wellness remains a top priority, making your home a sanctuary of peace and happiness for both of you.

TECHNIQUES TO ENHANCE MENTAL WELL-BEING

Ever noticed how a well-timed belly rub or a game of fetch can turn a grumpy pup into a wagging bundle of joy? It's no secret that our canine companions thrive on attention and activity, but maintaining their mental well-being often goes beyond the occasional scratch behind the ears or a romp in the park. Just like us, dogs need a balanced diet of engaging activities and calming routines to stay mentally sharp and emotionally stable. Let's dig into some wholesome strategies to keep your dog's tail wagging happily.

First up, let's talk about behavioral enrichment activities. These are not your average games of fetch; they are thoughtfully designed to challenge your dog's problem-solving skills and stimulate their senses. Imagine setting up a treasure hunt for your dog inside your home. You could hide treats in various nooks or in puzzle toys that require manipulation to access the goodies. Each successful find not only rewards them with a tasty snack but also a mental victory lap. Another fantastic activity is teaching them new tricks or commands. This could be anything from learning to open a door with a touchpad to sorting toys by color. Yes, dogs can learn colors! These activities make daily life more interesting for your dog and can significantly enhance their cognitive functions.

Routine might sound dull to thrill-seekers, but in the canine world, it's the bedrock of stability and security. A consistent daily routine keeps the guesswork out of your dog's day, providing a comforting predictability that many dogs find reassuring. Regular feeding times, walks, and quiet periods help create a structure that can alleviate stress and anxiety. It's like having a reliable schedule that tells them when it's time to play, time to eat, and time to chill. This predictability helps reduce behavioral issues such as excessive barking or chewing, which often stem from anxiety or confusion about what's expected of them.

Now, for those moments when the world seems a bit too much for your furry friend, relaxation techniques can be a game-changer. One effective method is massage. Yes, dogs love massages too! A gentle rubdown can soothe your dog's nerves and improve their circulation, providing a physical and emotional calming effect. Soft music designed for canine ears and calming scents like lavender can also create a serene environment for your dog to unwind. Picture this: after a long day, you and your dog are relaxing in a softly lit room, soft music playing in the background, and a gentle scent of lavender in the air—sounds pretty blissful, right?

However, there are times when even the best routines and relaxation techniques might not suffice. That's when professional behavioral therapy comes into play. Dogs, like people, can have deep-seated anxieties or stress disorders that require professional intervention. A veterinary behaviorist specializes in these issues and can offer therapies that go beyond basic training. They can work with your dog to address fears, phobias, and aggressive behaviors in a safe, controlled manner. Think of them as the dog psychologists whose expertise can help unravel complex behavioral puzzles. Consulting a professional is not about admitting defeat in your training abilities; it's about doing what's best for your dog's emotional and mental health.

Incorporating these techniques into your dog's life doesn't just enhance their well-being; it deepens the bond you share. Each activity, whether a brain-teasing game or a calming massage, is an opportunity to connect with your dog and provide them with a richer, more fulfilling life. It's about giving them tools to cope with the stresses of the world and enjoy a contented, happy existence by your side. So, the next time you see your dog getting a bit anxious or stressed, remember that a little creativity in their routine might just be the spice of life they need.

THE IMPACT OF SOCIALIZATION ON BEHAVIOR

Think of socialization as the secret sauce that can transform a shy, wary puppy into a confident, happy dog who sees the mail carrier as a friend rather than a foe. The benefits of proper socialization are akin to the layers of an onion, each peel revealing more advantages. At its core, effective socialization reduces fearfulness. This isn't just about preventing your dog from hiding under the table during a thunderstorm; it's about helping them feel secure in their daily environment, whether they are navigating the bustling streets on a walk or encountering new guests at home. As their confidence blooms, so does their ability to handle new or unexpected situations. A well-socialized dog is like a well-traveled explorer, each new experience adding to their repertoire of skills and knowledge, making them adaptable and stress-resilient.

Now, let's break down the art of socializing your dog, shall we? It's not just about exposure; it's about controlled, positive exposure. For puppies, this journey begins the moment they step paw into your world. Introducing them to a variety of people—kids, adults, the elderly, people of different ethnicities—as well as to other animals, sounds, and environments lays a foundation as robust as steel. Start with short, sweet encounters that leave your puppy wanting more. Always pair these introductions with positive experiences; a treat here, a gentle pat there, or a cheerful voice to make that new experience a joy rather than a fear. It's like setting up a series of mini-adventures where each one ends with a little party, making your puppy associate new experiences with fun times.

Transitioning to adult dogs, especially those who might not have had the benefit of early socialization, requires a mix of patience and strategy. Think of it as teaching an old dog new tricks, but instead of tricks, you're teaching them to trust. Begin with low-stress environments and gradually introduce more challenging scenarios. For instance, if your adult dog is uneasy around other dogs, start by observing from a distance where they feel safe, gradually decreasing that distance over time. Pair each step with something positive, like their favorite treat or a fun game, to build positive associations. Remember, the pace should be dictated by the dog's comfort level; pushing too hard can backfire, turning what should be a positive experience into a stressful ordeal.

The role of socialization in preventing behavioral issues cannot be overstressed. Many common behavioral problems, such as aggression, fear-based behaviors, and excessive barking, often stem from inadequate socialization. By exposing your dog to a wide range of experiences in a controlled, positive manner, you're essentially equipping them with the tools they need to interact with the world around them confidently. This proactive approach is like putting money in the bank; it's an investment in your dog's future behavior that pays dividends by preventing potential problems down the line.

Socializing your dog is one of the most impactful things you can do for their overall well-being. It opens up a world where things that might once have scared them become parts of an exciting adventure to be explored. Whether you're working with a bubbly puppy or a more reserved adult dog, the principles of patience and positive exposure can transform the way they view the world. It's about more than just making your dog friendly; it's about giving them the confidence to face the world without fear, fully enjoying the rich, joyful life they deserve alongside you.

RECOGNIZING SIGNS OF DEPRESSION IN DOGS

Have you ever noticed a day when your usually sprightly pup didn't rush to greet you at the door? Maybe they didn't even wag their tail much when you offered them their favorite treat. It's easy to chalk it up to an off day, but what if it's something more? Just like us, our canine companions can experience periods of depression, where the zest for life they once had seems to diminish. Recognizing the signs of canine depression is crucial because, unlike us, our dogs can't verbally express how they feel. They rely on us to read their non-verbal cues and help them when they're feeling down.

Symptoms of depression in dogs can sometimes be subtle and gradually build up, making them easy to miss if you're not observant. Changes in eating and sleeping habits are common red flags. A dog that suddenly loses interest in food or begins to sleep more than usual could be showing signs of depression. Similarly, a decrease in activity level is a telltale sign. If your once energetic pup now prefers lying in their bed over a game of fetch, it's worth considering why. Another significant indicator is a lack of interest in play or interaction. Dogs are naturally social creatures, so when they start withdrawing from interactions with you or other pets, it's often a sign that something is amiss.

Understanding what might be causing your dog's depression is the next step. Often, the trigger can be a significant change in their environment or life. The loss of a companion, whether it's a fellow pet or a human family member, can hit dogs particularly hard. They form strong bonds, and the absence of a loved one can leave them feeling lost and sad. Major changes like moving to a new home, changes in the family dynamic, or even alterations in their daily routine can also lead to depression. Additionally, chronic pain, which might not be immediately apparent, can be an underlying cause. Conditions like arthritis can make your dog feel lethargic and unwilling to engage in activities they once enjoyed.

When it comes to treating depression in dogs, the approach can vary depending on the underlying cause but generally involves a combination of increased interaction, environmental changes, and possibly medical intervention. Boosting your daily interactions with your dog can have a profound effect on their mood. More walks, play sessions, and cuddle times can help strengthen your bond and alleviate their loneliness. Sometimes, simply spending quiet time together, letting them know you're there, can provide immense comfort.

Environmental changes can also play a significant role in lifting your dog's spirits. This might include creating a more stimulating home environment with new toys or safe spaces that they can call their own or regular visits to new, exciting places. If your dog's depression stems from the loss of a companion, introducing a new pet can sometimes help, though it should be done with careful consideration of the dynamics and personalities involved.

In cases where depression is linked to physical pain or is particularly severe, consulting with a veterinarian is crucial. They can assess whether medical intervention is needed, such as pain relief for underlying health issues or even antidepressants in extreme cases. It's important to closely monitor your dog's response to any treatments and maintain regular check-ups to ensure they're on the path to recovery.

Supporting a dog with depression requires patience, empathy, and attentiveness. It's about being there for them, just as they've always been there for you, and making adjustments to your life together to help them feel better. Remember, you know your dog better than anyone else, so trust your instincts. If you notice changes in their behavior, don't wait to seek help. Early intervention can make a significant difference in your dog's mental health and overall well-being. By providing ongoing support and monitoring their behavior, you can help guide your furry friend back to a happier, more active life.

CREATING A STIMULATING ENVIRONMENT FOR YOUR DOG

Imagine your home as a playground, where every room offers a new adventure, every corner a surprise waiting to be discovered. This doesn't just make life more fun for your pup; it actively engages their mind, keeping them sharp and content. Let's start with the magic of interactive toys and puzzles. These aren't your average squeaky toys; they're the canine equivalent of Sudoku or a good mystery novel. From puzzle boards that challenge them to move pieces for treats to interactive gadgets that respond to your dog's actions, these toys encourage problem-solving and can keep them busy for hours. Think of a toy that dispenses a little treat only after your dog figures out how to roll it in just the right way. It's not just play; it's a brain workout, and it's a joy to watch your dog's gears turn as they figure out the game.

But the environment involves more than just what's on the floor; it includes how the space is set up. Designing your home in a way that encourages exploration can be incredibly stimulating for a dog. Consider creating different levels they can reach, like a small pet-safe platform or steps to their favorite window lookout. You can hide treats in these spots occasionally to give them a reason to explore. Incorporating feeder toys that make them work for their food can also turn mealtime into an engaging activity that satisfies their natural foraging instincts. It's about creating an environment where they can use their natural abilities in fun, healthy ways.

Now, let's talk about shaking up their routine. Just like humans, dogs can get bored with the same old schedule, day in and day out. Introducing regular changes to their routine can spice up their daily life and keep them guessing. Maybe one day, you take your walk at a brisk, energetic pace, and the next, you make it a leisurely stroll with plenty of time to sniff and explore. Or perhaps you switch up the games you play together, replacing fetch with a hide-and-seek game using their favorite toys. These variations can help keep their minds engaged and their bodies active, preventing the boredom that often leads to destructive behaviors.

Community and social interactions play a pivotal role in your dog's mental stimulation and social skills. Regular playdates with other dogs, trips to the dog park, or simply walking in busy areas where they can meet new people and pets can greatly enhance their social skills and mental health. Each new interaction is a learning opportunity, helping them become more adaptable and comfortable in various situations. It's also a chance for them to burn off some energy and make new friends, which is just as important for their emotional well-being as it is for ours.

In creating a stimulating environment for your dog, you're doing more than just keeping them entertained. You're providing them with the mental and physical challenges that are essential for a healthy, happy life. You're helping them develop the skills they need to navigate the world with confidence and curiosity. So take a look around your home from your dog's perspective and start thinking about what changes you can make to turn it into a stimulating, exciting space. Whether it's through smart toys, a creatively arranged living space, a varied routine, or plenty of social interaction, each element you introduce will help your dog live a fuller, more engaging life.

As we wrap up this chapter on creating a stimulating environment for your dog, remember that the goal is to enrich their daily life and foster a deep, satisfying bond between you two. By providing a variety of mental and physical activities, you ensure your dog remains active, engaged, and above all, happy. These strategies not only prevent behavioral issues but also enhance the overall quality of life for your furry companion. As we move forward, we'll explore the importance of health and nutrition in further supporting your dog's lifestyle, ensuring they not only have fun but also stay healthy and well throughout their lives.

AGING AND SENIOR DOG CARE

P icture this: your once sprightly pup, who used to turn your backyard into a racetrack, now ambles along, taking in the scenery with a more dignified pace. Yes, time spares no one, not even our furry companions. As they step into their golden years, their care routine needs a bit of tweaking, especially when it comes to their diet. It's a bit like adjusting the seasoning in a stew to get that flavor just right—too little salt, and it's bland, too much, and it's overwhelming. Let's make sure we get it just right for our aging pals, ensuring their later years are as golden as they deserve.

NUTRITIONAL ADJUSTMENTS FOR AGING DOGS

As dogs age, their metabolism slows down, much like a sleepy Sunday morning when it's hard to get out of bed. This reduced energy expenditure means their caloric needs decrease—feeding them the same amount you did when they were bounding with puppy energy might lead to weight gain. Obesity in senior dogs isn't just about waistlines; it can exacerbate health issues like arthritis, diabetes, and heart disease. It's crucial, then, to adjust their caloric intake to suit their more sedentary lifestyle. Think of it as resizing their meals to fit their current life chapter—smaller portions but still packed with all the nutrients they need.

Now, speaking of nutrients, senior dogs have some specific needs. Their diet should be rich in fiber to help keep their digestive system running smoothly—think of fiber like a gentle broom sweeping through a dusty hallway, keeping everything clean and tidy. Antioxidants are another key player. They help combat the effects of aging at the cellular level, much like a splash of anti-aging cream helps keep our skin youthful. Foods rich in antioxidants can support their immune system and ward off diseases. And let's not forget about omega fatty acids, which are like the oil in a creaky door hinge for their joints. These nutrients help reduce inflammation and keep their joints supple, making it easier for them to get up and go chase those squirrels (at a more dignified pace, of course).

But what if your senior dog turns up their nose at their food? Appetite issues are common in older dogs, whether from diminishing senses of smell and taste or other underlying health problems. To tackle this, consider warming their food or adding a bit of broth to enhance the flavor and aroma, making it more appealing. It's like jazzing up a dinner party dish with a dash of spice or a sprinkle of herbs, turning it from meh to mouthwatering.

Regular dietary assessments with your vet play a crucial role in keeping your senior dog's diet on track. Just as we might adjust our diets as we age—cutting down on those midnight snacks or adding more leafy greens—our dogs need their diets tweaked to suit their changing health needs. These check-ups can help catch any potential issues early and keep your senior dog's tail wagging at mealtime.

Navigating the dietary needs of your aging dog ensures they continue to thrive in their senior years. By adjusting their diet to reduce caloric intake, focusing on essential nutrients, making their meals more palatable, and regularly assessing their dietary needs, you provide them with the support they need to age gracefully. It's about adapting to their pace, making small changes that make a big difference, and ensuring that their twilight years are filled with as much joy and health as possible.

MANAGING MOBILITY AND JOINT HEALTH IN SENIORS

As our beloved dogs reach their senior years, you might notice they're not as quick to jump up for a treat or might hesitate before tackling the stairs. It's a bit like watching your favorite childhood hero slow down; it tugs at the heartstrings. But here's where we can step in and make a world of difference. Joint health becomes paramount as dogs age, and thankfully, there are a plethora of ways we can support our furry friends to keep them moving comfortably.

Let's talk about supplements first, like glucosamine, chondroitin, and MSM—these are the unsung heroes when it comes to joint health. Think of glucosamine as a tool that helps build and repair cartilage, the cushion between bones in a joint. As dogs age, this cushion wears down, which can lead to discomfort and reduced mobility. Adding glucosamine to your dog's diet is akin to putting extra padding on your running shoes—it makes each step more comfortable. Chondroitin works hand-in-hand with glucosamine, helping to enhance its effects and further support cartilage repair, while MSM, a natural pain reliever, helps soothe sore joints, acting like a gentle, natural balm that eases joint pain. Incorporating these supplements can help maintain your senior dog's bounce in their step, allowing them to keep up with younger pals at the park.

Switching gears to physical therapy, this is not just for humans recovering from injuries. For senior dogs, physical therapy can be a game-changer. It's like yoga and a good stretch rolled into one, tailored for your dog. Specific exercises can help maintain muscle mass and enhance joint mobility, keeping those legs strong and agile. Techniques such as passive range of motion exercises gently move the joints through their normal range, promoting flexibility without causing pain. Then there's hydrotherapy—imagine your dog paddling in the water, supported and soothed by its buoyancy, which reduces stress on painful joints while providing a good workout. Regular sessions can significantly enhance your senior dog's mobility and quality of life.

Now, about navigating their environment—this can become challenging as dogs age. Mobility aids such as ramps or steps can be a true blessing. Think of a ramp as a gently sloping path that invites your senior dog to join you on the sofa without the daunting challenge of a jump. It's about adapting your home to meet their needs, ensuring they can still enjoy their favorite sunbathing spot by the window or easily step into the car for a ride to the park. Similarly, harnesses that support lifting can help you help them, providing a gentle lift for stairs or vehicles or just to navigate a tricky path on your daily walk.

Lastly, let's consider routine modifications. Just as we might swap a high-impact aerobics class for something gentler as we age, adjusting your dog's routine can mitigate the wear and tear on aging joints. Shorter, more frequent walks can keep your senior dog active without overstraining their joints. Soft bedding can work wonders, too, offering a cozy, supportive spot for rest and recovery. It's about making small adjustments that yield significant benefits, allowing your senior dog to navigate their day without undue strain on their bodies.

Supporting the mobility and joint health of your senior dog involves a blend of supplements, physical therapy, thoughtful use of aids, and routine tweaks. It's about creating an environment that acknowledges their changing needs, providing them with the support they need to continue enjoying life, just at a slightly slower pace. With these tools, your senior dog can continue to explore the world with comfort and joy, making the most of their golden years alongside you.

COGNITIVE DECLINE: PREVENTION AND CARE

As our beloved dogs enter their golden years, it's not just their bodies that show signs of aging; their minds can too. If you've noticed your old friend seems a bit more forgetful, maybe standing at the wrong door to go out, or they don't get as excited about their favorite toy, they might be experiencing cognitive decline. It's like when you walk into a room and forget why you're there, but for them, it happens more frequently. Recognizing these signs early can make a world of difference in managing their condition and ensuring their twilight years are comfortable and filled with love.

Cognitive decline in dogs can manifest in various ways, such as disorientation, changes in sleep patterns, and a noticeable decrease in interaction with family members. Perhaps your once social butterfly now prefers solitude or doesn't greet you with the same enthusiasm. These changes can be subtle at first, but as they progress, they become more apparent. It's crucial to observe these changes without immediately dismissing them as just "old age." Keeping a mental or even a written log can help you track these shifts in behavior, providing valuable information when discussing with your vet.

Environmental enrichment plays a pivotal role in managing cognitive decline. Just like us, dogs need mental stimulation to keep their minds sharp. Introducing new toys that challenge them or revisiting old games can help. Puzzle toys that require them to solve problems or toys that engage their sense of smell can provide mental workouts. Scent games, where you hide treats around the house for them to find, can be particularly beneficial. They not only stimulate their brain but also keep them physically active. Gentle, consistent interaction with family members can also help. Regular, gentle play sessions, short walks, and even talking to them about your day can help keep their mind engaged.

Diet also plays a crucial role in managing cognitive health. Dietary adjustments, particularly those that boost brain function, can be beneficial. Antioxidants help combat oxidative stress, a key component in cognitive decline. Foods rich in antioxidants include blueberries, spinach, and carrots, which can be added to their meals in moderation. Supplements like medium-chain triglycerides, commonly found in coconut oil, have been shown to improve brain energy metabolism and can be a helpful addition to their diet. It's important, however, to discuss any dietary changes or supplements with your vet to ensure they're safe and appropriate for your dog's specific health needs.

Knowing when to seek veterinary advice is crucial. If you observe any signs of cognitive decline, a vet visit is in order. Early intervention can slow the progression and even improve quality of life. Your vet might suggest specific therapeutic diets, medications, or lifestyle changes that can help manage the condition. Regular check-ups become even more important as your dog ages, as these visits can help catch and address not just cognitive issues but any other age-related conditions that might arise.

Navigating the challenges of cognitive decline in your aging dog requires patience, love, and a proactive approach. By staying alert to the signs, enriching their environment, adjusting their diet, and maintaining regular veterinary care, you can help manage their symptoms and ensure their senior years are filled with as much joy and comfort as possible. After all, they've spent their lives bringing happiness into yours; it's only right we do everything we can to return the favor as they grow old.

COMFORT MEASURES FOR AGING DOGS

Creating a sanctuary for your aging dog isn't just about adding a few extra pillows or turning up the heat. It's about reimagining their living space to cater to their evolving needs, ensuring each day is spent in comfort, not in coping. Think of it as remodeling a house when a new baby arrives; adjustments are necessary to make it safer and more comfortable. For senior dogs, this might mean installing non-slip flooring to prevent those heart-stopping slip-and-slide moments. Rugs or yoga mats strategically placed can offer much-needed traction as they navigate their favorite spots around the house.

Next, consider their sleeping area. Your dog might have once enjoyed leaping onto a high bed or snuggling deep into a plush couch, but as they age, these simple pleasures can become daunting tasks. Orthopedic dog beds, placed in accessible, draft-free spots, can provide joint support and make lying down or getting up less painful. Temperature control is also crucial; older dogs are more susceptible to temperature extremes. A chilly room might exacerbate arthritis, while an overly warm space can lead to discomfort and dehydration. Think about adding a heated bed for chilly nights or a cooling mat for those warm summer days, keeping their body temperature just right for comfort and health.

Pain management in senior dogs is as much an art as it is a science. It starts with recognizing the signs of discomfort—maybe they're not as eager to climb stairs, or perhaps they hesitate before jumping off the curb. When these signs appear, it's essential to consult with your veterinarian about pain relief options. Medications can certainly help, but there's also a world of alternative therapies that can complement traditional treatments. Acupuncture, for instance, has gained traction in the veterinary world for its effectiveness in managing pain and enhancing mobility. It involves inserting tiny needles into specific points on the body to release endorphins and stimulate nerves, muscles, and connective tissue. It's all about restoring balance and alleviating discomfort, allowing your dog to relax more fully.

Massage therapy is another gentle way to help manage your senior dog's pain. It's not just about giving your dog a spa day but about enhancing their well-being. Regular massage can increase circulation, help manage pain, reduce stress, and even improve the range of motion. Picture this: your gentle strokes not only deepen the bond you share but also help soothe their tired muscles. Plus, it's a serene moment to connect with your aging friend, providing them with reassurance and comfort.

Monitoring the quality of life is perhaps the most heart-touching aspect of caring for a senior dog. It's about being deeply attuned to their needs and happiness. Are they enjoying their daily activities? Do they still delight in meals and treats, or have they lost interest? Assessing their quality of life involves observing their behavior for signs of pain, discomfort, or withdrawal. It also includes regular check-ins with your vet to discuss their health and make adjustments to their care plan. This ongoing evaluation helps ensure that the measures you're taking are enhancing their life, not just extending it. It's a delicate balance, one that requires compassion, attention, and an unwavering commitment to their dignity and happiness. As they age, our role as pet parents is to adapt our care to meet their changing needs, ensuring their golden years are filled with warmth, love, and comfort.

8.5 END-OF-LIFE CARE AND DECISION MAKING

When the twilight years of our beloved dogs approach, it's not just a time of reflection but also one of crucial decision-making that underscores our deep love and responsibility towards them. Understanding palliative care is essential during this period. Think of it as a comforting blanket over their shoulders, not aimed at curing but at ensuring comfort and dignity. Palliative care focuses on managing symptoms that cause discomfort and stress, whether they are physical, like pain and nausea, or emotional, like anxiety. The goal is to maintain the best possible quality of life for as long as life remains. This might involve adjusting medications to ease pain, offering more comfortable bedding to soothe arthritic joints, or simply ensuring that their favorite treats are on hand when they feel like eating.

Deciding on euthanasia is perhaps one of the most heart-wrenching decisions a pet owner can face. It's a decision that carries the heavy burden of a pet's life, balanced against the desire to prevent unnecessary suffering. When the quality of life has deteriorated significantly—where the pain is unmanageable, or the joys of their days have slipped away—it may be time to consider this final act of love.

Discussing this option with family and your veterinarian can provide different perspectives and emotional support that help you make a well-considered decision. It's important to evaluate their quality of life objectively, which can sometimes mean setting aside our own desires to keep them with us a bit longer, focusing instead on what is best for them.

Grieving the loss of a pet is a process as individual as the bonds we share with them. For many, a pet is not just a companion but a family member whose passing leaves a palpable void. Acknowledging the grief, allowing yourself to feel it, and seeking support are all steps towards healing. Many find solace in support groups dedicated to pet loss, where shared experiences and understanding provide comfort. Counseling services can also offer a structure through which you can process your feelings and start to heal. Remember, grieving is a testament to the love shared and an important step in honoring their memory.

Honoring and memorializing a pet can be a deeply personal act that reflects the special bond you shared. Creating a memory book filled with photos and favorite moments can be a therapeutic activity that celebrates their life. Planting a tree or a garden in their memory offers a living tribute that grows and blossoms—a natural symbol of the ongoing impact they have on your life. Some might choose to hold a small memorial service, gathering friends and family who knew your pet to share stories and say goodbye. These acts of remembrance can provide comfort and closure, helping to ensure that the love you shared continues to resonate.

Navigating the final chapter of a dog's life with compassion and courage ensures that their last days are as loving and comfortable as possible. It's a profound responsibility, one that honors the journey shared and the unconditional love they've offered throughout their lives. As we close this chapter on caring for aging dogs, we transition into exploring how best to continue our lives while cherishing the memories of those who have left paw prints on our hearts.

EMERGENCY PREPAREDNESS AND FIRST AID

Imagine this: You're enjoying a perfect sunny day at the park with your furry best friend, playing fetch, and basking in the joyful chaos of wagging tails and frisbees. Suddenly, your pup lets out a yelp, limping back to you with a paw raised. Your heart drops. What do you do? Well, that's where a well-stocked canine first aid kit becomes your unsung hero, transforming a moment of panic into a calm, controlled response. Think of it as your Batman utility belt; it's better to have it and not need it than to need it and not have it!

BUILDING A CANINE FIRST AID KIT

Essential Items

A canine first aid kit isn't just a bunch of medical supplies thrown together in a box; it's a carefully curated collection that anticipates your dog's most urgent needs. At its heart are the essentials: gauze for wrapping wounds or muzzling an injured dog (only if necessary, since we all know our pups can be dramatic at times), adhesive tape for securing the gauze (because that bandage isn't going to hold itself up), antiseptic wipes for cleaning boo-boos, and a digital thermometer (trust me, trying to figure out if your dog has a fever without one is as puzzling as solving a Rubik's cube in the dark).

But let's not forget about tweezers for those pesky splinters or ticks, saline solution to flush out dirt or debris from the eyes, and scissors with rounded tips to cut hair or bandages safely. And, of course, a pair of gloves to keep things sanitary and prevent any contamination. It's like packing for a vacation; you want to be prepared for anything without lugging the entire house along.

Specialized Supplies

Just like us, every dog is unique with their own set of quirks and needs. This is why having specialized supplies tailored to your dog's specific health requirements is crucial. For instance, if your dog has allergies, including their specific medication, it can be a lifesaver in preventing a reaction from turning severe. Or, if you're in an area known for snakes or other venomous creatures, having a venom suction extractor could literally be a lifesaver. It's about understanding the environment and your dog's personal health landscape—mapping it out can be as intricate as planning a road trip across the country.

Storage and Accessibility

Storing your canine first aid kit is just as important as what's inside it. You'll want to keep it in a cool, dry place but easily accessible in an emergency—think of it like storing chocolate; you want it out of the sun but within easy reach when you need a pick-me-up. Ensure it's out of reach of children and, importantly, curious noses that might think the kit is a new chew toy. Consider also having a smaller, portable version for your car or backpack when you're on the go because emergencies don't have the courtesy to always happen at home.

Regular Updates and Maintenance

Maintaining your first aid kit is like checking the oil in your car; it needs to be done regularly to ensure everything's running smoothly. Check the expiration dates on all items periodically and replace any supplies that have been used or have expired. It's also a good idea to refresh your knowledge of first aid practices now and then—knowing what to do with the tools at your disposal is just as vital as having them. You wouldn't want to find out you forgot how to use the fire extinguisher right when you need to put out a fire, right?

Building and maintaining an effective canine first aid kit might seem like a daunting task, but it's an invaluable resource that can make all the difference in an emergency. Just like carrying an umbrella, it's not about being pessimistic but being prepared. So, take a little time to assemble these essentials, familiarize yourself with their uses, and keep your kit updated. That way, you can enjoy all the sunny days and unexpected adventures with your four-legged friend, knowing you're prepared for whatever comes your way.

BASIC FIRST AID PROCEDURES FOR DOGS

When you're faced with a doggy emergency, time seems to stand still, and every second counts. That's why knowing how to swiftly assess your dog's condition in an emergency is akin to being the conductor of a very tense orchestra. You need to quickly understand what's wrong to make the right calls. Start by checking the vital signs: heart rate, breathing, and gum color. To check the heart rate, place your hand on the left side of the chest; you should feel the heartbeat. Count the beats for 15 seconds and multiply by four to get the beats per minute. Normal ranges can vary, but typically, it's between 60 to 140 beats per minute for dogs, depending on size and breed. Next, observe their breathing. Are they panting heavily, struggling, or breathing too slowly? Normal is 10 to 35 breaths per minute. Lastly, check the gums. They should be pink, not white or blue; this indicates good blood circulation. If they press on their gum, the color should quickly return once they release it.

Handling wounds properly is crucial to prevent infection and further injury. Let's say your dog has stepped on something sharp during your adventurous hike. First, you'd calm them down with soothing words and gentle strokes—yes, talking to them like the brave little trooper they are. Then, clean the wound. Rinse it with a saline solution to flush out dirt and debris. If saline isn't available, clean water will do. Pat the area dry with a clean cloth. Apply an antiseptic wipe gently around the wound to kill any germs lurking about. If the wound is bleeding, apply pressure with sterile gauze to stop it. Once the bleeding is under control, wrap the wound lightly with gauze and secure it with adhesive tape. Remember, the wrap should be snug but not a tourniquet—tight enough to stay on, loose enough to slip a finger under.

Now, if you ever find your dog unresponsive, knowing how to perform CPR (Cardiopulmonary Resuscitation) could literally be a lifesaver. Before you start, ensure they really need CPR: check if they're breathing and if they have a pulse. Lay them on their right side, straighten their head to open the airway, and pull the tongue forward past the canine teeth. If no breathing, give rescue breaths by closing the dog's mouth and breathing directly into their nostrils every 5-6 seconds. Next, perform chest compressions. The technique varies slightly depending on the size of the dog. For large dogs, compress the chest at the widest part, while for smaller dogs or puppies, you might compress just over the heart with one hand. Press down about one inch for smaller dogs and up to three inches for larger dogs. Compressions should be quick and firm, with 100-120 compressions per minute. Alternate between compressions and rescue breaths.

Shock is a life-threatening condition often caused by trauma, severe blood loss, or allergic reactions, and recognizing it could be crucial. Symptoms might include weak pulse, shallow breathing, and cold limbs. If you think your dog is going into shock, keeping them warm and calm is paramount. Cover them with a blanket to conserve body heat and keep the environment quiet and soothing. Elevate their hind legs slightly to help blood flow to the vital organs. Speak to them in a calm, reassuring tone—let them know you're there, handling things. Then, get to a vet immediately. Shock can worsen rapidly, and they'll need professional medical intervention.

Mastering these first aid techniques gives you a toolkit not just packed with skills but with confidence. It prepares you to handle those heart-racing moments with a cool head and a steady hand. Whether it's a minor wound from an overzealous adventure or a more severe condition like shock, knowing what to do in those first few moments can make all the difference. And while we all hope never to use these skills, having them ready is part of the commitment we make when we bring these loving creatures into our lives. Your readiness ensures that your furry friend has the best chance possible in any emergency, reinforcing the unspoken pact of trust and care that defines your bond.

RECOGNIZING AND RESPONDING TO POISONING

Imagine you're enjoying a serene afternoon in your backyard, watching your dog frolic among the flowers, a picture of pure joy. Suddenly, your dog begins to act strangely, pawing at their mouth, drooling excessively, or even starting to vomit. Your heart races—could they have ingested something harmful? The garden, much like the inside of your home, hosts a myriad of substances that, while seemingly benign, can pose serious risks to your curious canine. From the chocolate cake left unattended on the coffee table to the beautiful yet toxic lilies adorning your garden, the hazards are plentiful and often hidden in plain sight.

Firstly, let's talk about the usual suspects in your home and garden that could turn a perfect day into a scary one. Foods like chocolate, grapes, and xylitol-containing products such as sugar-free gums are well-known no-nos for dogs. Each of these can cause anything from gastrointestinal disturbances to severe poisoning. Then there are plants—lovely to look at but dangerous to nibble. Lilies, tulips, and sago palms, to name a few, can all be toxic if ingested. And let's not forget about common household chemicals; antifreeze, rat poison, and even some types of cleaners can be lethal if your dog decides to take a taste. It's like setting up a home security system; you need to know what could potentially harm your beloved pet and where these dangers lurk.

Now, spotting the signs of poisoning early can make all the difference. Symptoms can range widely depending on the toxin involved but typically include vomiting, diarrhea, severe lethargy, and sometimes more alarming signs like seizures or collapse. If you observe your dog exhibiting any unusual behaviors, such as excessive drooling, pawing at the mouth, or sudden changes in their mental state, it's crucial to act swiftly. These signs can escalate quickly, and every moment counts.

In the event you suspect your dog has ingested something toxic, the first step is to assess the situation calmly but quickly. If it's safe and you are certain of what they have consumed, you might need to induce vomiting to prevent further absorption of the toxin. However, this is not always recommended, as some substances can cause more harm on the way back up. For instance, if the ingested material is sharp, acidic, or alkaline, inducing vomiting could complicate the situation significantly. It's akin to knowing when to douse a fire with water and when to use a fire extinguisher; using the wrong method can exacerbate the problem.

Your immediate action should be to contact your veterinarian or a pet poison control center. These professionals can provide guidance based on the specific poison involved. Keep the substance container or a sample of the plant or material your dog ingested at hand, as it could be crucial for determining the best treatment strategy. Your quick and informed response can be the difference between a minor incident and a life-threatening situation.

Reaching out to professionals right away not only ensures you're taking the proper steps but also preps your vet for the situation if you need to rush your dog to the clinic. They might advise you on how to safely transport your pet, what symptoms to watch for en route, and how to provide supportive care until you can get professional help. It's like having a skilled guide when you're navigating treacherous waters; their expertise can steer you to safety.

In the whirlwind of managing a poisoning incident, remember your composure and quick thinking are invaluable. Just as you would prepare for any other emergency, knowing ahead of time what substances are toxic, recognizing the signs of poisoning, and understanding how to respond can save precious time—and potentially, your dog's life. It's about being proactive, informed, and ready to act, ensuring the safety and well-being of your faithful companion in any situation.

HANDLING HEATSTROKE AND COLD INJURIES

Let's talk about the weather—specifically, how it can be more than just a small talk topic when it comes to your furry friend. Dogs, much like us, can suffer from the extremes of heat and cold, but unlike us, they can't just change their coat or grab a drink whenever they fancy. That's why understanding how to prevent and respond to heatstroke and cold injuries is crucial. It's like being your dog's personal meteorologist, and emergency responder rolled into one.

Starting with heatstroke, a condition that can sneak up during those glorious sunny days meant for fetch and fun. It's vital to remember that dogs don't sweat through their skin like we do. They rely primarily on panting to cool down, and sometimes, that just isn't enough. To prevent heatstroke, never, and I mean never, leave your dog in a parked car. It's not a sauna session, and even with the windows down, the temperature inside a car can skyrocket to deadly levels in minutes. Always provide ample shade and fresh water when you're out enjoying the sun. Whether it's a tree, a tent, or an umbrella, make sure your pup has a cool retreat from the sun's rays. And if it's particularly scorching, consider setting up a kiddie pool or a sprinkler for them to splash around in—think of it as their personal mini water park.

Now, recognizing heatstroke early can be the difference between a minor incident and a medical emergency. Signs to watch for include excessive panting that doesn't resolve with rest, drooling more than usual, reddened gums, and a body temperature above 104°F. Your dog might also seem less responsive or even disoriented. If they start vomiting or collapse, it's past the warning stage and well into emergency territory. If you suspect heatstroke, acting quickly is crucial. Move your dog to a shaded or air-conditioned area immediately. You can help lower their body temperature by applying cool (not cold) water to their body. Focus on areas with less fur and the skin underneath, like the belly. Offering them small amounts of cool water to drink can also help, but don't force it, as they might not be able to swallow properly.

Switching gears to the chillier side of things, cold injuries like frostbite and hypothermia are also serious risks, especially for breeds that aren't built for cold or sudden cold snaps. Prevention here is all about proper attire and timing. When the temperature drops, consider a doggy coat or sweater, especially for short-haired breeds or smaller dogs that lose heat quickly. Limit the time spent outside on freezing days, and always wipe down your dog's paws when coming back inside. This not only removes any ice and snow but also any potentially harmful chemicals like road salt or antifreeze, which can be toxic if licked off.

Should your dog get too cold, the first signs might be shivering, slowed movements, or looking for places to burrow for warmth. In severe cases, like hypothermia, they might become sluggish or unresponsive. If you notice these signs, warming them up gradually is critical. Wrap them in blankets, possibly warmed in the dryer for extra coziness, and give them a warm (not hot) place to rest. You can offer warm fluids to drink, but similar to heatstroke, ensure they can swallow properly first to avoid choking. Always remember, whether it's a sweltering summer day or a frosty winter evening, keeping your dog safe from the whims of Mother Nature is a year-round commitment. Just like you'd slather on sunscreen or bundle up before heading out, taking a moment to consider your dog's needs can ensure that every day is as safe as it is fun.

PREPARING FOR NATURAL DISASTERS WITH PETS

When the skies darken and the winds pick up, your first thought is to protect your family—and that includes the four-legged members. Preparing for natural disasters with pets in tow isn't just about having an extra bag of kibble; it's about crafting a plan that considers all the what-ifs, ensuring that when you need to act, it's with clarity and quickness. Imagine this: a storm is brewing on the horizon, and while it might be a bit nerve-wracking, you feel a wave of calm knowing you've prepared a comprehensive disaster plan that includes your pets.

Creating a disaster preparedness plan often starts with the basics—knowing your evacuation routes and the locations of pet-friendly shelters. But it delves deeper. You need to consider each step you would take from your door to a safe location. This might involve practicing driving the route to ensure it's clear and that you know alternative paths should the need arise. Also, compile a list of pet-friendly places along the way, including hotels or shelters, because the last thing you want is to be turned away during a stressful time.

Next, let's pack an emergency kit specifically for your pets, which is like their little suitcase packed with all the essentials. Start with food and water—enough for at least three days. Pack it in sturdy containers, and don't forget a manual can opener if you use canned food. Include medications with clear instructions and a first aid kit. Comfort items like a favorite toy or blanket can also make the situation less stressful for your pet. Think of this kit as a grab-and-go bag that lives by your front door; it's there to scoop up on your way out, ensuring your pet has everything they need to stay safe and healthy.

Identification and documentation are your best friends in times of chaos. Ensure your pet wears a collar with an ID tag that includes your current contact information. Microchipping is another layer of security that can make all the difference if you and your pet get separated. It's a simple procedure that can be done during a regular vet visit. Along with ID, keep a file with important documents such as vaccination records and medical history. Store these digitally, if possible, or in a waterproof container. This way, if you need to prove ownership or provide medical information, everything is at your fingertips.

Training your pet for evacuations can turn a potential panic into a smooth operation. Start with getting them comfortable with their carrier or crate. Leave it out in your home with the door open, placing treats and favorite toys inside to encourage exploration. Take short drives if your pet isn't used to traveling in a vehicle, gradually increasing the time as they become more comfortable. Practice evacuation drills with your pet, using the carrier and loading them into the car. This helps ensure that when the time comes, they won't be overwhelmed by the sudden flurry of activity.

By integrating these strategies, you create a safety net woven with the threads of foresight, preparation, and love. It means when the winds howl and the earth shakes, your focus can remain on what truly matters—keeping your entire family, paws and all, safe from harm. As we wrap up this chapter on emergency preparedness, remember that this isn't just about responding to what nature throws your way, but proactively embracing the responsibility of pet ownership. It's about ensuring that come rain or shine, high waters or shaking grounds, you and your furry companions are ready to face whatever comes your way, together.

Moving forward, in our next chapter, we'll explore the realms of pet insurance and healthcare—a guide to navigating the financial aspects of pet care, ensuring your pet's health is safeguarded through all of life's ups and downs.

BUILDING AND MAINTAINING THE BOND

Remember the first time your dog looked up at you with those big, soulful eyes, and it felt like they could see right into your heart? That moment likely marked the beginning of an incredible bond, one that would grow stronger with each shared experience, from belly rubs to long walks and, yes, even those early morning wake-up calls with enthusiastic, tail-wagging urgency. Building and maintaining a bond with your dog is not just about companionship; it's about creating a deep, trusting relationship that enhances both of your lives. This chapter delves into the subtleties of strengthening that connection through touch, voice, and mutual respect—elements that turn your interactions from routine to remarkable.

THE ROLE OF TOUCH AND VOICE IN BONDING

Power of Physical Contact

Touch is one of the most potent tools in your bonding arsenal. It's the warmth of a gentle stroke, the comfort of a snug cuddle, and the joy of a playful wrestle. Each contact with your dog reinforces your bond, communicating safety, affection, and trust. Consider how a simple petting session can soothe a nervous pup or how a belly rub can turn your dignified dog into a goofy, leg-kicking mess of happiness. These interactions are not just pleasant; they're foundational, building layers of trust and affection that permeate your relationship.

Massages can elevate this connection further, turning your touch into a therapeutic tool. Just as humans benefit from the relaxing strokes of a massage, dogs too can find comfort and relief in gentle, rhythmic motions. This not only eases their physical tensions but can significantly reduce anxiety, strengthening their emotional trust in you. It's like finding a silent language through which you can communicate your care and commitment, deepening the bond without a word spoken.

Using Voice Effectively

Your voice is another powerful bonding tool, capable of conveying everything from approval to reassurance. Dogs are incredibly attuned to our vocal tones. A soft, soothing tone can calm a fearful dog, while a cheerful, enthusiastic one can encourage a hesitant pup during training sessions. The consistency of your voice commands also plays a crucial role. Imagine the confusion if sometimes "sit" is a command and other times it's part of a casual conversation. Clear, consistent command tones help your dog understand what you expect of them, reducing frustration on both ends.

Here's a little trick: vary your vocal pitch to keep your dog engaged and responsive. Higher pitches often excite and encourage, while deeper tones might convey seriousness or disapproval. It's like being the conductor of an orchestra, where your voice is the baton guiding your dog through the symphony of daily life, each note a cue for a new part of the routine.

Training with Positive Reinforcement

Incorporating touch and voice into training sessions can dramatically enhance the effectiveness of your teaching efforts. Positive reinforcement, such as a pat on the head along with a cheerful "good dog!" when your dog sits or stays on command, not only makes the training enjoyable but also reinforces their perception of it as a positive, rewarding experience. This method strengthens your bond, turning training sessions into opportunities for mutual enjoyment and appreciation.

Recognizing and Respecting Boundaries

Just as in any good relationship, recognizing and respecting boundaries is crucial. There will be times when your dog might not feel like being touched, perhaps when they're scared, not feeling well, or simply not in the mood. Pushing interaction in these moments can lead to resentment or discomfort. Learning to read your dog's body language—a tucked tail, averted gaze, or tensed body can all be signs of discomfort—helps you respect their space. Respecting these boundaries doesn't weaken your bond; rather, it communicates a deep level of understanding and respect for their feelings and comfort.

In every gentle touch, every soothing word, and every respected boundary, you are building a bridge of trust and affection with your dog. This connection becomes the foundation of a relationship characterized by mutual respect, deep affection, and an unspoken understanding that no matter what, you are there for each other. Through these simple, everyday actions, you turn the ordinary into something extraordinary, transforming routine interactions into the threads that weave the rich, beautiful tapestry of companionship with your dog.

REGULAR GREETING AND ITS BENEFITS BEYOND APPEARANCE

Think of grooming not just as a chore or a necessity but as a golden opportunity to bond with your furry friend. Picture the scene: you, armed with a brush and treats, and your dog, perhaps a bit bewildered at first but soon relaxing into the gentle rhythm of your strokes. These regular grooming sessions become more than just a way to keep your dog looking good—they transform into moments of connection that both you and your dog will grow to cherish.

Grooming sessions are the perfect time to reinforce your bond with your dog. They learn to trust you with their body, which, in the dog world, is a big deal! It's a trust that says, "I believe you have my best interests at heart," which, let's be honest, you absolutely do. This routine becomes a predictable, enjoyable part of their day, something they look forward to. For you, it's a chance to slow down and focus solely on your dog, making them feel loved and cared for. It's a win-win: your dog gets a sparkling coat, and you both enjoy quality time together.

But grooming isn't just about looking good; it's also a critical component of your dog's health regimen. Each session gives you a chance to check your dog over for any bumps, lumps, or skin irregularities. Think of it as a casual yet thorough health inspection that can catch potential issues before they become serious. You feel their skin for signs of ticks or fleas, you comb through their fur, looking for mats that might be causing discomfort, and you keep an eye out for any signs of infections or inflammations. It's proactive health-care that keeps your dog in top shape, allowing you to address issues promptly with your vet.

Now, let's talk about making grooming a stress-free experience for your pup. If you start when they're young, they'll grow up seeing grooming not as something to be endured but as a normal, even enjoyable part of life. Begin with short, positive sessions. Praise them frequently, keep treats on hand, and always end on a high note. If your dog is older and perhaps not so keen on the idea of being brushed or bathed, patience is key. Gradual introduction combined with lots of positive reinforcement can work wonders. It's about creating a narrative in your dog's mind that grooming equals good things, like treats and a gentle, loving touch.

The emotional comfort grooming can offer to a dog is profound. In the wild, grooming is a communal activity that reinforces social structures and bonds within the pack. When you groom your dog, you're tapping into this deep-seated instinct. It's soothing for them, a process that feels inherently right and comforting. On days filled with thunderstorms or fireworks, a gentle grooming session can be just the thing to help calm a nervous dog. It's a reminder that they're not alone, that their pack—aka you—is right there with them, offering safety and comfort through the simple act of grooming.

As you make grooming a regular part of your life with your dog, you'll find it's about so much more than just keeping them neat and tidy. It's a ritual that strengthens your bond, enhances their well-being, and enriches your shared life. Every stroke, every snip, every gentle cleansing is a message of love and care, a tangible demonstration that they are a cherished part of your family.

CELEBRATING YOUR DOG'S LIFE: BIRTHDAYS AND GOTCHA DAYS

Imagine this: a cake topped with a dog biscuit candle, a tail wagging faster than the speed of light, and a chorus of "Happy Birthday" sung slightly off-key. Celebrating your dog's birthday or gotcha day isn't just about the fanfare; it's about acknowledging the joy and unconditional love they bring into your life every day. Creating memorable traditions on these special days strengthens your bond and gives your furry friend a sense of inclusion and importance in the family unit. Why not start with something as simple as a special meal? Picture your dog's delight at finding a slice of dog-safe cake at the end of their dinner or the excitement of a special chew toy that comes out only on these special days. These small gestures make your dog feel cherished and truly part of your family's special moments.

Now, let's talk about turning these personal celebrations into a community affair. Hosting a dog-friendly party can be a thrilling event not just for your dog but for your friends and their canine companions as well. It's like the social highlight of your dog's year! Picture a backyard filled with wagging tails, an obstacle course, and perhaps a kiddie pool for those who fancy a paddle rather than a sprint. These gatherings are not just fun; they're a fantastic way for dogs to socialize and for you to share tips and stories with other dog lovers. Alternatively, organizing a group outing to a local dog park or a dog-friendly beach can also offer a fun, relaxed setting for everyone to get some fresh air and celebrate together. It's about creating a sense of community and sharing the love and joy that each dog brings into our lives.

Reflecting on milestones during these celebrations is equally important. Each birthday or adoption anniversary marks another year of growth and shared experiences. Think back over the past year and consider all the adventures you've had, the challenges you've overcome, and the quiet moments that have filled your days. Maybe it was the first time your dog bravely conquered the stairs, or the afternoon you both got caught in the rain, turning a simple walk into a muddy, unforgettable escapade. These reflections not only deepen your appreciation for your relationship but also remind you of the journey you're on together. It's a celebration of the past, present, and the many years of companionship yet to come.

Documenting these moments creates a treasure trove of memories that you can look back on with joy. Whether it's a photo album filled with pictures of each birthday, a box of small keepsakes like their first collar or a favorite toy, or even a digital slideshow that chronicles their life, these memories become a narrative of your life together. On days when you need a smile, or when you're celebrating another year together, these memories are a reminder of the bond you share. They tell a story not just of a pet and an owner but of a family.

As these celebrations weave into the fabric of your life, they become more than just days on a calendar. They are heartfelt reminders of what it means to have a dog: a life enriched by joy, companionship, and love. Celebrating your dog's special days is a reflection of the gratitude you feel for their presence in your life and an affirmation of the many wonderful moments yet to come.

In wrapping up, remember that each wag, each woof, and each wonderful moment with your dog builds a story—a story of friendship, growth, and unconditional love. Celebrating their birthdays and gotcha days is just one of the many ways you can express your love and make them feel as special as they make you feel every day. As we close this chapter and look forward to the next, consider these celebrations as milestones not just in your dog's life but in your journey together, enriching the profound connection you share.

CONCLUSION

As we draw the curtains on this comprehensive guide, it's essential to reflect, not just on the content, but on the journey itself. Owning a dog, as we've explored together, is not merely about having a pet; it's about welcoming a new member into your family whose presence reshapes your world in the most extraordinary ways. This book has guided you through the nuanced dance of dog ownership, from selecting your canine companion to nurturing their health and happiness throughout their life stages.

Together, we've navigated the broad spectrum of care necessary for our furry friends. We've discussed how to choose the right dog for your lifestyle, the importance of balanced nutrition, and the benefits of consistent training. We've stressed regular exercise and proactive healthcare, including both traditional veterinary care and holistic alternatives. We delved into the mental and behavioral wellness of our dogs and acknowledged the special considerations needed as they age gracefully by our sides.

Each chapter was crafted to arm you with knowledge and strategies to enhance the life of your beloved dog. From puppyhood to their golden years, the journey requires patience, consistency, and an abundance of love, elements that transform not only the life of your dog but yours as well.

Now, I encourage you, the reader, to take these insights into your daily life. Apply the lessons learned and watch as your relationship with your dog blossoms into something even more beautiful. Remember, the efforts you invest in their well-being will circle back, enriching your own life with unmatched companionship, unconditional love, and the pure joy that only a dog can bring.

For those eager to connect with others who share this passionate journey, I urge you to reach out. Join online forums, participate in local dog clubs, or attend community events. There is a whole community of like-minded dog lovers out there, and together, the support and shared experiences can make the journey even more rewarding.

I want to extend a heartfelt thank you for joining me on this journey. Your commitment to giving your dog the best possible life is a testament to the depth of your heart. As you continue this rewarding path, remember that the challenges you face are but stepping stones to a richer, more joyful life with your four-legged friend.

Lastly, I invite you to share your own stories and experiences. Whether through social, a review of this book, or a personal message, your insights can help foster an ongoing dialogue that inspires and educates. Let's continue to support each other in this fulfilling endeavor of dog ownership.

Thank you for choosing to walk this path with me. Here's to the many adventures and heartwarming moments ahead with your beloved canine companions!

REFERENCES

- *Choosing the Right Breed for Your Lifestyle* https://www.akc.org/expert-advice/vets-corner/choosing-right-breed-lifestyle/
- *Which Is Best For You: Adopting an Adult Dog vs Puppy* https://www.whole-dog-journal.com/training/which-is-best-for-you-adopting-an-adult-dog-vs-puppy/
- *Finding a Responsible Dog Breeder: What to Look For* https://www.akc.org/expert-advice/dog-breeding/signs-of-a-responsible-breeder/
- *What is a Dog Health Certificate? Why is it Important?* https://www.vet-sentry.com/what-is-a-dog-health-certificate-why-is-it-important/
- *Vet-Approved Homemade Dog Food Recipes* https://www.thesprucepets.com/homemade-dog-food-recipes-5200240
- *How to Read a Dog Food Label* https://www.webmd.com/pets/dogs/features/how-to-read-a-dog-food-label
- *The Benefits of Omega-3 and Omega-6 for Dogs* https://www.purina.ca/articles/dog/nutrition/benefits-omega-3-and-omega-6-dogs
- *Food Allergies in Dogs* https://vcahospitals.com/know-your-pet/food-allergies-in-dogs
- *Top 10 Effective Dog Training Methods: A Complete Guide ...* https://theanimalcare.org/dog-training-methods/
- *The 13 Best Interactive Dog Toys for Mental Enrichment* https://www.thesprucepets.com/best-interactive-dog-toys-8363714
- *10 Common Dog Behavior Problems and Solutions* https://www.thesprucepets.com/common-dog-behavior-problems-1118278
- *Assistance Dogs International* https://assistancedogsinternational.org/
- *Dog Exercise Needs By Breed (Basic Guide & Time Chart)* https://fairmountpetservice.com/Blog/pet-services-blog/dog-walking/dog-exercise-needs-breed-guide-chart/
- *5 Benefits of Dog Agility Training* https://www.thewildest.com/dog-behavior/dog-agility-training
- *22 Ways to Play with and Exercise Your Dog Indoors* https://petcube.com/blog/indoor-dog-exercise/
- *Following a Weight Loss Plan for Dogs* https://vcahospitals.com/know-your-pet/creating-a-weight-reduction-plan-for-dogs

- *USDA Approves Merck Animal Health's NOBIVAC® NXT ...* https://www.merck.com/news/usda-approves-merck-animal-healths-nobivac-nxt-canine-flu-h3n2-the-first-and-only-rna-particle-technology-vaccine-for-canine-influenza/
- *Pet dental care* https://www.avma.org/resources-tools/pet-owners/petcare/pet-dental-care
- *Titer Testing for Dogs: An Alternative to Annual Vaccinations* https://www.thewildest.com/dog-health/titer-testing
- *guide-to-congenital-and-heritable-disorders.pdf* https://www.hsvma.org/assets/pdfs/guide-to-congenital-and-heritable-disorders.pdf
- *Acupuncture For Dogs: Everything You Need to Know* https://www.akc.org/expert-advice/health/acupuncture-for-dogs/
- *Veterinary Herbal Medicine: A Systems-Based Approach* https://www.ncbi.nlm.nih.gov/pmc/articles/PMC7151902/
- *How Massage Can Help Your Dog* https://www.akc.org/expert-advice/health/massage-can-help-your-dog/
- *CBD Oil for Dogs: What You Need to Know* https://www.akc.org/expert-advice/health/cbd-oil-dogs/
- *Expert Tips to Help Soothe Your Dog's Anxiety* https://www.akc.org/expert-advice/training/soothe-dog-anxiety/
- *Why Socialization is So Important for Dogs* https://wagwalking.com/wellness/why-socialization-is-so-important-for-dogs
- *Depression in Dogs: Symptoms, Causes, Treatments ...* https://www.webmd.com/pets/dogs/features/depression-in-dogs
- *Interactive Dog Toys for Mental Stimulation – P.L.A.Y. - PetPlay* https://www.petplay.com/collections/enrichment-toys
- *Senior Dog Nutrition and Supplement Tips* https://www.akc.org/expert-advice/nutrition/nutrition-and-supplements-for-senior-dogs/
- *Arthritis in Dogs: How to Treat and Manage Pain ...* https://www.akc.org/expert-advice/health/dealing-with-canine-arthritis/
- *Management of Dogs and Cats With Cognitive Dysfunction* https://todaysveterinarypractice.com/neurology/management-of-dogs-and-cats-with-cognitive-dysfunction/
- *Senior Dog Food: Meeting Aging Canines' Nutritional Needs* https://www.webmd.com/pets/dogs/features/senior-dog-food
- *Dog First-Aid Kit Essentials: What to Include For Injuries ...* https://www.akc.org/expert-advice/lifestyle/dog-first-aid-kit-essentials/
- *How to Perform Pet CPR | Red Cross* https://www.redcross.org/take-a-class/cpr/performing-cpr/pet-cpr

- *Poisoning: First Aid and After Care for Your Dog* https://wagwalking.com/wellness/poisoning-first-aid-and-after-care-for-your-dog
- *Pet Disaster Preparedness Recovery* https://www.redcross.org/get-help/how-to-prepare-for-emergencies/pet-disaster-preparedness.html
- *Healing Effects of Animal Touch & Animal Presence* https://www.awionline.org/sites/default/files/publication/digital_download/AWI-LA-Magic-of-Touch.pdf
- *Positive reinforcement training* https://www.humanesociety.org/resources/positive-reinforcement-training
- *The Health Benefits of Dog Grooming* https://www.doglyness.com/blogs/news/the-health-benefits-of-dog-grooming
- *10 Ways to Celebrate Your Dog's Gotcha Day* https://www.bringfido.com/blog/how-to-celebrate-your-dogs-gotcha-day/